D1433801

No Cake, No Jam

MARIAN HUGHES

No Cake, No Jam

LONDON NEW YORK SYDNEY TORONTO

Printed and bound in Great Britain by
Mackays of Chatham PLC, Chatham, Kent

Contents

ONE

Brimstone

Standing at the bottom of the large staircase, I lifted my arms as I gazed up at the sun that shone through the faceted glass in the high, domed skylight above the stairwell. All the colours of the rainbow cascaded about me and I felt a powerful sense of harmony and joy.

I was three years old.

I remember sitting on a long form, packed tight with little girls all dressed in blue smocks, savouring the delights of demerara sugar on hard, stale bread, and revelling in a sense of triumphant satisfaction when the last portion was consumed.

Vividly I recall an occasion when older girls coaxed me into putting my fingers against a gadget on the wall. Seeking to please, I did so, and received an electric shock. I remember the intense curiosity with which I viewed the seemingly dead metal plate which blended into the decayed, old wall.

I'd been in an institution, the Lady Montague Home for Infants, a place where I felt total security, since six months after my birth in 1931.

All too soon the calm, ordered atmosphere changed. Strange men and fur-clad old ladies came looking round the Home. There were tears, and a sense of foreboding that seemed to weigh on all the grown-ups. Everything was packed on to lorries and we girls were paraded in the courtyard. The Founder had passed away. We were to be taken to another, much larger, institution. I can still remember the looks of pity given us, and the uneasiness I felt.

On this day, I was told that I would be joining two older sisters and a brother. Their existence had passed out of my memory, and I received this information with apprehension. My developing sense of individuality felt threatened.

We left in a long crocodile. The little ones were carried. It seemed a very long walk from Brixton to Stockwell. But finally we arrived and stopped before a pair of enormous iron gates, in front of and behind which a lodge extended. On either side of the gates was a high wall which seemed to surround the whole establishment.

After a consultation at the gates, we entered Spurgeon's Orphanage.

The buildings of the Orphanage resembled an army barracks: great blocks of grey, soot-dirtied stone with barred windows. We stood in silence and trepidation as we surveyed the hideous structures that surrounded the terraced lawns and playgrounds.

My sisters, standing nearby, were swiftly introduced to me. I warmed to Dorothy as she gently took my hand. But before I had a chance to appraise either of them properly, they were gone.

My arrival coincided with the night the Crystal Palace burned. We were woken by excited cries of wonder as girls climbed up at the windows. The sky was lit up with great glory, and I fell asleep visualising my beautiful cascading dome, and thought of a splendid palace of light, and grieved a little.

In time I discovered that the edifice opposite the gates was the chapel. The bleak, two-storey, barrack-like buildings, which seemed to go on forever, ran parallel, on either side of the gates, the whole dimly lit by gas and poorly heated in winter. There were constant draughts, accounting for the whispering and moaning sounds which terrified us. Upstairs, there were vast dormitories off interminable corridors; downstairs, the school, the dining-rooms and the workrooms, and the bathroom containing six baths off the boiler house alongside the huge, steaming laundry.

Girls and boys were totally separated except in the chapel where I first felt the impact of religion. A God who watched my every move! Hell fire and damnation! The evil of our bodies! Eternal judgement and eternal retribution!

We were perhaps five hundred girls and boys, nurtured on a form of Calvinism, together with an adequate diet and the most elementary of the three Rs.

On Sundays, the chapel reverberated with the sounds of children singing, boys and girls separated by the long aisle. While I was aware of the boys, I showed them not the slightest interest. The older girls referred to them spitefully. I did not even wonder which was my brother in the sea of grey-uniformed, close-cropped heads. I merely observed their close regimentation. They always moved with military precision and were docile and quiet, never looking towards the girls. I was told that tufts of hair were left on top of their shaved heads so they could be grasped.

Preachers would come and hold forth for all they were worth, pleading for missionaries among the children while not belittling too much the general training of a career in domestic service. To this end the whole institution was scrubbed, polished and almost boiled every day. Clothes were washed, mended and folded. Beds were made meticulously. Shoes were shined, and woe betide anyone who did things sloppily.

But religion wasn't all bad. There were beautiful hymns, with wonderful lines that could express almost every emotion. Words and phrases ran like rivers around my head, feeding vague longings. I sang with joy, but occasionally words conjured up frightening images and stirred powerful visions of an awesome, mystical element which held a strange appeal for me.

Education was, outside the humdrum of my well-ordered life, an uncertain affair. I don't ever remember learning to read or going through the torture of many of the girls who stumbled over the repetitious happenings of families brought to life in dog-eared reading books. Many of us had no experience of home life. These books brought a grief of longing that almost engulfed me.

Some of the new girls would cry for 'Mummy'. I, with others, would laugh at them, and call them sissies. The soft lap and the strong, safe, gentle arms of a mother were things I couldn't bear even to think about.

I couldn't remember ever being touched, except for punishment. I had dim recollections of standing rigidly in Lady Montague Home and having my buttons done up and my shoes tied by impatient adults who made efforts not to touch me and who I dreaded would inadvertently do so. Often these episodes would induce me to flinch which somehow invited a sharp slap. I was soon a master of the minor art of quickly dressing myself.

Aspects of the Orphanage had a brutalising effect on many of the girls. There were unwritten laws, cliques and hierarchies. It didn't do for us younger children to assume privileges we were not entitled to. Consequently there was a lot of bullying. If members of the staff were aware of it, they chose to ignore it; perhaps they were unable to cope with it.

Millicent, my elder sister, hardly figured in my life. I was wary of her and treated her with the same respect as I did the other older girls. Dorothy was different; she doted on me and would protect me from unkind attentions. So, with this champion behind me, I suffered less than some.

The girls were allowed to converse only at playtime, and then there seemed little time for communication. The call of 'Don't stand there chatting' often came from Miss Mirk, who handed out skipping ropes of various sizes, encouraging us to spin in and out of them at great speed. Miss Mirk had a hare-lip, which intrigued me, but I would charitably pretend not to notice. Dancing exhibitions would include acrobatic feats and dear Miss Mirk would have tears of pride in her eyes which she would dab with the point of a large handkerchief, hiding her lip and giving herself an appearance of grandeur. She was very tall and straight, her blue-black hair tied up in an enormous bun on top of her head. She had large, kind, clear eyes and a long, straight nose. Observing her thus, I could understand her habit of draping the handkerchief at rare times of recognition.

'Marian Hughes! No cake! No jam!'

Miss Marriott's voice rang out some twenty feet below me as I hung from the centre of the ceiling.

Encouraged by a ring of girls, I had shinned up the wall and had 'walked' hand over hand hanging from the gas pipe which was now very slowly dropping from its fixtures.

'Mattresses!' screamed Miss Marriott, her skinny arm pushing at a group of girls gathered about her.

'Run! *Run!*' she cried.

Off they went, caught up with the frenzy in her voice.

Miss Marriott promptly knelt to pray.

About to speak, I merely gasped, for the slightest movement produced an ominous creak and a downward lurch of the pipe. Surprised at my predicament, I thought only of the punishments ahead. Well, they could beat me to death and I wouldn't bat an eyelid! I wouldn't care!

In a great flurry, mattresses were hurled beneath me.

'Jump!' yelled Miss Marriott.

'No! I won't! I can't!' Suddenly I felt afraid.

Miss Marriott's hysterics had got through to me; besides, a couple of the girls were crying.

'Fetch Matron!' shrieked Miss Marriott.

Matron was the ultimate threat. Matron was never seen. I had no idea who she could be.

The shouting below me faded. Suddenly, there appeared 'my Angel'.

'My Angel' was a face. She would appear fleetingly in door-ways or at mealtimes. She had a look of love and approval, which nobody else seemed to notice. Once she looked directly at me and smiled. Such a marvellous smile. I secretly called her 'my Angel', and prayed to heaven to catch glimpses of her.

She walked across the floor unhurriedly. She stooped to adjust the mattresses, then walked away.

'Don't go! Oh please don't go!' I cried.

I felt the pipe giving way. 'My Angel' glanced upwards, gently smiling, turning my fear away. I let go and was unharmed.

Astonished, I discovered that 'my Angel' was indeed the dreaded Matron.

She took my hand and led me silently past the girls who feigned gasps of dread about my fate. But there were to be no punishments. I was taken to her private rooms. Her sitting-room was cosy, cluttered and seemed to be ablaze with light. A tray arrived, with the most delicate china tea things upon it. It was magical.

'What is your name, child, and how old are you?' Her voice was as sweet as her smile.

'I am Marian Hughes and I'm seven.' I was direct but without my usual air of defiance.

'Seven? My goodness! Are you happy, Marian Hughes?' There was a gentle hint of amusement in her smile.

'Yes, Miss,' I whispered, overawed.

The incident was like a dream and no reference was made to the awful act of wickedness that had brought me to this paradise.

At tea-time on Sunday those on punishment would have their names announced. These children were allowed just plain bread and scrape which passed along the narrow table seating thirty girls. Their knives were removed and they had to fix their eyes upon their bread until the others were served.

I was rarely presented with an amber or red blob of jewelled jam shining vividly against the white enamel plate. Instant saliva flooded my mouth as I passed these offerings along. These delights would be followed by a slice of currant cake which other girls, sometimes spitefully, would ogle in exaggerated ecstasy. I would bear this outrage with defiant dignity.

After the episode of climbing up the gas pipe, I was sent, escorted by a 'big girl', to bed, where I lay going over my past misdeeds. I had poisoned other girls on vinegar (sorrel) leaves, berries and other natural products in an enactment of surviving forty days and forty nights in the wilderness. I had unravelled my Sunday best jumper. Dismantling a bathroom tap, with tools left by a plumber, I had caused extensive flooding. I had defaced God's holy work by cutting out pictures of Jesus, the scissors having been slyly secreted from the sewing-room. These incidents were preceded by many more, lost in memory, for which I had received many a savage beating from those whose calling was to guide my immortal soul.

It was only five o'clock, sunny and warm outside, and I felt an increasing desire to wander. Miss Goodenough (who wasn't), had just popped in (threatening goodness knows what if I dared even to turn over in bed), so it seemed a safe moment to venture out.

Creeping along the corridor, I heard crying coming from the sick bay. Betty Leggatt, a big girl, was lying in bed softly sobbing.

'Betty, what's the matter?'

'What are you doing here?'

'Never mind that. Why are you crying?'

'My leg's bad and it hurts so much!'

As she lifted back the covers, an ugly odour arose and I shrank back. 'Oh Betty, you smell awful!'

Betty renewed her sobs.

She had hurt her shin jumping over forms some weeks ago and it had never healed. Her leg was bandaged, her foot was swollen and black.

That was the last time I saw her. I was devastated by the news that Betty had 'gone to Jesus'.

'Oh Betty! *Betty*!' I yelled and burst into tears.

I was promptly hauled out of line, given a violent shaking, and fiercely ordered to behave. But grief overwhelmed me and once more I received the punishment of an early bedtime.

Betty's short life and sudden death created in me a sense of nameless fear. She'd been one of the few older girls who had been protective towards me and was known for her kindness. Certain that Betty was now in Heaven, I knew, were I to die, I'd surely go to Hell.

School involved sewing and the incessant rolling of plasticine. Bible stories abounded as well as exploits of the Founder of the Orphanage (who took children from the *dregs* of society!). The greatness of the British Empire, the idea of ships and vast seas, filled me with images. I ended up day-dreaming and staring up at the windows, oblivious of my surroundings.

My fantasies were sharply interrupted. Miss Bryden hauled me out of my seat and dragged me to the front of the class.

'I've long come to the conclusion that you are an imbecile!' she exclaimed. Then she addressed the other children. 'She may be articulate, but did you see her smiling at nothing? Even muttering? We will no longer put up with her!'

It seemed that it had already been decided that I was to be sent to the sewing-room where I could dream away while making use of my talents. I would be in the class of the dreaded Miss Frampton whose secret cruelties were never witnessed by the staff. (I had myself seen under-matrons stamping on the bare feet of children, and pulling their ears until a popping sound was heard.)

Miss Frampton's diction was perfect and she looked directly at me when she spoke. That prompted respect.

She beamed, and I found it difficult to understand the sullen faces of the row of girls seated in absolute silence on a long bench under the window.

'Come now, child, I hear you do this work beautifully?'

This, with a smile, was all the encouragement I needed. Utterly confident of my own abilities, I sat down on the edge of the form, pretending not to notice the resentful glances as I forced the other girls to shuffle along, further restricting their movements. I proceeded to work the hem given me.

Now and then I looked up to encounter Miss Frampton's benign smile. Eager to please, I worked as fast as I could, producing, I was positive, the finest hem in the land.

'Please, Miss, I've finished!' I cried, anticipating acclaim.

I jumped up and thrust the work at Miss Frampton who after the most perfunctory glance, threw it down. Then, drawing herself up, she gave me the most vicious slap around my head so that I was flung forcefully to the floor. I rolled over, picking up my work as I returned to the bench where the other girls, with slight smiles of gratification, shoved up, giving me very little room.

'Marian Hughes! You do not address me! You put up your hand when you have finished your work and you keep silent. We do not have these outbursts in this room. I was led to believe you were a girl of exceptional talent. You are not. But I will not give up on you, I do not give up on a child. You will not look at me. You at all times will look at your work or will fix your eyes on the floor. Is that understood?'

'Yes, Miss,' I whispered.

'You will unpick that hem and do it properly.'

Astonishment and fright soon gave way to immense anger. I started picking at the seam while Miss Frampton walked up and down, occasionally examining the girls' work. As her shoes stopped in front of me I felt my face flush. I was trembling with rage.

I lifted my head and, with all the arrogance I could muster, I gazed at Miss Frampton.

Miss Frampton whacked me round my head which sent two or three of the girls off balance. She returned to her desk.

I was sitting next to Gladys Watts who squeezed my hand and whispered, 'Don't!'

But by now a battle had started and whatever it cost me I was determined to win.

Miss Frampton walked towards me.

Not a word was spoken.

The next savage blow caused my left eye almost to close and far-away bells to ring in my head.

Gladys put her arm protectively round me, a brave act, but Miss Frampton did not notice. She looked deranged, uncertain and desperate. The next time she did not strike but picked me up and shook me interminably, then threw me back on the bench.

'Leave her alone!' screamed Gladys, putting an arm in front of me. But I pushed her away and waited with a sense of triumph for Miss Frampton's now halting steps.

This time it looked as if she would not return. I sprang up and yelled, 'You cannot hurt me! You cannot hurt me!' and, to the horror of all present, I thrust the needle through my own hand. With disgusting defiance, I blew my nose on the fine linen and flung it away.

Miss Frampton crumpled into her chair, her head in her

hands. I felt a strange elation which was marred by the difficulty I experienced in removing the needle from my hand.

From that moment Miss Frampton ignored me, directing other girls to give 'that child of the devil' work to do.

For a while, I became a heroine. I had driven the old dragon to lose control, and until that moment Miss Frampton's control had been spoken of in whispers. No one had ever dared to challenge her. I warmed to the adulation but it passed.

Gladdy-what-what, as we called her, continued to try to protect me from my excesses. She was not successful.

Something was happening, something unusual. School and sewing were abandoned and the staff huddled together in urgent, whispered discussion. People from outside the Orphanage measured our heads without explanation and enquired about our health. There was an air of expectancy which was contagious.

I had no idea what it was all about until my sister Dorothy rushed over to me in the playground with a look of alarm.

'There's going to be a war!' she announced uncertainly.

A wave of unspeakable excitement, mixed with fear and joy, swept through the girls. Something extraordinary was about to happen! What, no one seemed to know. Speculation and hysteria abounded. I hung around the older girls to glean information.

'Hey you! Scat!' commanded Joan Dawson, a big ugly girl feared by the little ones.

Not put off, I dared to persist, sure that this clique of girls would know what was going on. I heard the words 'Germans' and 'evacuation'. Every Friday, we lined up in the lavatories for a dose stirred in the bottom of a mug of brown stuff we called 'Brimstone' which produced the most awful colic. We were told that this medication would 'assist the evacuation of germs in the bowels'. Disappointed and no wiser, and fearing that 'Brimstone' would be dished out more frequently, I started being cheeky.

I shook the back of the bench.

'You're a lot of germs!' I said, looking directly at the dreaded Joan Dawson. I resented their secrecy.

'Did you hear that child?' cried skinny Jane Blare, aping an adult's tone.

'I bet you've all got nits!' I ventured, trying to think of something awful.

Joan Dawson scowled, jumped up and made a grab for me, but like quicksilver I darted away and stuck out my tongue.

'Scabby face, scabby face . . . smellies!' I sang.

I was caught by some of the girls, flung into the air, and the next thing I knew Joan Dawson was sitting astride me and I was gasping for breath. By then the commotion had produced a semi-circle of anticipation. Feeling pretty desperate, I stared defiantly into glowering eyes. For a brief moment a subtle change seemed to occur, a fleeting glance of apology or regret. That hesitation saved me from a battering. From far across the playground Dorothy had streaked and delivered my attacker a mighty kick square on her nose. Poor Joan Dawson let out a bellow, covered the bleeding injury with her two hands, got up and ran. Dorothy stood, white and shivering, shocked at the result of the impact.

Dorothy was a 'good girl'. She was loved by the staff and respected by everyone. Rickets had left her with a double curvature of the spine and she wore thick-lensed, steel-rimmed glasses which almost hid her deep blue eyes. She was kind and wise. I got sick of being told 'I wish you were more like your sister Dorothy!' Yet I felt a constant tinge of regret at being unable somehow to follow her example.

'What was going on here?' demanded Dorothy.

'She was calling us names,' one of them whined.

Without waiting for further explanations Dorothy lightly

smacked me. I burst into tears, then revelled in the subsequent comforting which consisted of assisted eye-drying and nose-blowing.

'You've got to be a good girl. I've found out what's happening. We're going to leave this place, all of us. I don't know where we're going but we'll all be together. They'll not split us up, ever!'

Very little of the outside world was known to me. In the Orphanage there were no newspapers, no books of any substance (except the Bible), no wireless or music (only hymns, songs of patriotism and simple piano works for dance exercises), no mirrors. Questions about our bodies were discouraged. I was told that the world was wicked as were our bodies.

I knew England to be the centre of the Empire and that children lived in families, with mothers and fathers, grandparents, uncles and aunties. I imagined every household with hordes of occupants, all loving. Somewhere there were evil people, but what form their wickedness took I had no idea. There were the King and Government, fishermen and farmers. Here in the Orphanage, the only men we saw were those who came to mend things, smelling of bonfires. There were also missionaries and preachers, and funny ladies who sang in a manner that struck me as extremely comical. One woman snorted on every intake of breath, causing us to fall about with laughter. Many of us suffered canings over this involuntary behaviour.

Flustered adults were rushing about ordering the big girls to empty cupboards and pack the contents into hundreds of tea chests which were then stacked in the playground. We younger girls were left to our own devices, whereupon we explored

13

forbidden territories in an orgy of unfettered and unaccustomed freedom.

We ate sandwiches in long rows on the lawns instead of having a set meal in the dining-hall. We sat on the green banks for ages. Girls were stood up in groups and taken to the lavatories.

One of my earliest achievements centred around the lavatory. Every morning we were sat upon seats in a row of open cubicles and were issued with scraps of newspaper. These we had to hold upside down so as not to be contaminated with the contents. Quickly able to read the upturned print, I was transported to the realms of magistrates' courts, China, dog-racing, the sale of property and a host of advertisements. We raised our hands to signify inspection by the under-matron, who would emit sounds of contentment or disappointment. The newspaper was appropriately used and the under-matron would manipulate the mysterious lever which would flush the lot. My satisfaction was supreme.

Having the habit of singing snatches of hymns in my head, for this event I chose a grand tune . . . 'Now my living has not been in vain! No-o my living has not been in vain!' and felt as merry as could be. I threw a lingering backward glance at the lavatories before being taken to the tables where we were ticketed, labelled and each issued with a cardboard box containing a gas-mask and another pack of sandwiches for the coming journey.

We seemed to wait for hours. Having already eaten the sandwiches, I now opened the lovely cardboard box and examined the curious-looking gas-mask. The long nose was most attractive, shining in the sun with blue-green iridescence. After a struggle, I managed to open the nose, the contents of which were passed round.

'Hey Marian, you've been sneaked on!' said a voice in a stage whisper behind me.

The pieces were hurriedly passed back and vainly I struggled to reassemble the gas-mask. Sure enough Miss Marriott was striding towards me. The girls either side made room for the onslaught. I lay back, trying to avoid the grasping hand. Miss Marriott grabbed my hair, propelling me upright, and dragged me to the other side of the lawn.

Behind a shed Miss Marriott, vigorously shaking me, proceeded to hit me: 'I . . . have . . . had . . . enough . . . of . . . your . . . tricks . . .' I wriggled away still clutching the gas-mask, which, though severely damaged, was to stay with me for the next few years.

We were led, crocodile fashion, through the gates to great, throbbing coaches. I climbed on with some trepidation. For many of us it was the first experience of being inside one of these chugging, explosive machines. We clung to each other, four to a seat, until it lurched forward, grating, roaring and sending rumbling vibrations through us in a terrifying manner. But this fright passed and soon the world opened up with so many wonders. Horses, cars, lorries, soldiers and shops. People, lots of people, all in a hurry. Trams, trolley-buses, houses and coloured lights.

'That must be the "green hill far away"!' cried one of the girls. Then, seeing the crows flying high over a field, we started to sing with great delight, 'Farmer Brown, Farmer Brown, watch them crows come flying down'.

Darkness fell. Exhausted by the singing and the day's excitement, we slept.

TWO

Radiation

Next morning I awoke to the magical sounds of birds singing. I was in a little room with only eight beds close together. Net curtains at the opened window billowed in the breeze over my bed, creating mystifying moire patterns. There was electric light, but now the sun was shining. The ceiling was decorated with floral mouldings. I thought it all beautiful. The repeated print on the wallpaper picturing an embracing young couple in mediaeval costume seated beneath a tree, fascinated me. I called them 'my people' and became fond of them.

We were about one hundred and twenty girls who had come to settle in this country mansion and the few cottages about the wooded estate encircling a large green. In this new congenial situation the atmosphere of the Orphanage seemed to change. Gone were many of the severe methods of treatment. A great cheer went up when we found that Miss Frampton and Miss Marriott had left us forever.

We spent a glorious first day in disorganised exploration of the house and grounds. I was overwhelmed by the canopy of trees, wild grasses, flowers and insects. I lay flat in a puddle, examining all kinds of minute crawling creatures. I was filled with wonder by the intricate and varied webs of the different spiders, the trapping of their prey; the sedate unconcerned pace of the snail compared with the manner in which the insects scurried hell-bent on some urgent errand.

About this time I realised that I had a mother.

Extraordinary letters came. They contained endearments and promises of 'one day . . .'. Indescribable longing overwhelmed me. I began to worship that mother. I could not bear the thought that I had so long been deprived of all knowledge of her.

Then she came to the Orphanage.

I couldn't reconcile this painted, over-plump, mangy-fur-coated woman with My Mother of The Letters.

Showing me clear disapproval, she said that she was sick of the reports of my bad behaviour that she constantly received. I felt totally rejected. I couldn't bring myself even to be near her. Dorothy seemed to chat with animation while I sat on one side, observing them sadly. I was fascinated by the slash of her bright red lipstick.

When she had departed, my anguish produced a sudden gush of tears.

Dorothy comforted me. 'Don't mind her, Marian! She's been very ill. She loves you, really she does.'

The letters still came and the apparition was soon forgotten. I dreamed of my adoring mother and, perhaps fortunately, she never visited again.

Now I started school. Released from the sewing-room, where I had learned with Miss Frampton to thread a needle with my eyes closed, new horizons opened up before me.

At eight-and-a-half years old, I had come late to the class-room, but I soon caught up with the still rather elementary curriculum offered. My reading above average and my writing improving, I was let into the secrets of rivers and oceans, maps and stars, basic arithmetic and history. My life was richer. I even managed not to be quite so wicked. Of course there were many

17

lapses. I just had to know how things worked. I was often caught dismantling something or concealing creepy-crawlies about my person, to the consternation of my betters.

Discovering poetry, enthralled by the flow and lilt of the language and the very special liberty of expression, I would spend long hours hidden away with a slim volume. Vague guilt would disturb me as I read uninhibited accounts of love, Godless fear and death. Through these works I became more aware of life, aspirations, and the need to be loved.

There were no mirrors available to us girls. But one day, I was given the privilege of cleaning a younger matron's room which included a dressing table with a fine looking glass above. Having caught glimpses of myself reflected fleetingly in the windows of the house, I became curious and sat in front of the mirror gazing at the image in front of me. My large, well-spaced, grey-blue eyes seemed a little fierce. I lifted the thatch of light blonde hair to reveal a high forehead and almost pointed ears. My nose was not worth considering, my jaw and chin just right, I thought. My lips turned up at the corners and my tongue must surely be the longest one in the Orphanage! Altogether, I liked my face, which was just as well since I was stuck with it. Deciding that I looked too serious, I smiled, transforming myself into a merry elf. I resolved to smile more often.

Girls came and went at the Orphanage. New girls often brought disease or infestations. In the old Orphanage they would have spent time in the sick bay to prevent outbreaks of illness, but here there was no space available. Often they were sad little creatures, frightened and shy.

Maisie Stocks sat snivelling and scratching her head, looking dejected. Her tear-streaked face was a picture of misery, and I felt deeply sorry for her. She was very dirty and I asked a matron standing nearby folding linen if she shouldn't be bathed.

'She won't.'

Maisie hugged herself. 'No! Git away from me!'

I took a jig-saw puzzle from the cupboard and proceeded to set it out on a low table.

'Have you done one of these?' I ventured, easing the table towards her chair.

'Dunno, no.' But Maisie looked a little curious. Before long we were chatting away and she turned out to be good at spotting which piece went where. I brought up the subject of the bath.

'Aw I don't know about a barf!' Maisie looked anxious again.

'Oh really, it's lovely,' I trilled joyously, 'like a warm blanket. And you'll smell nice and sweet and look pretty.' I took Maisie's hand. 'Say you will? For me?'

'I've never 'ad a barf!'

I held her hand up with mine. 'There! Isn't my hand pretty?' Maisie examined her own dirty fingernails. Quickly I added, 'Besides, there's lots of things you haven't had, isn't there? You're going to have to be clean.' Almost in despair, I blurted, 'Jesus wants you to be clean!'

'Who's Jesus?'

'Jesus washed all your sins away!' I cried with enthusiasm.

'Never 'ad sins!'

'Sins is all the bad things you think and do. It says in the Bible that cleanliness is next to Godliness. So you have to wash!' I tried again. 'Jesus loves you!'

''E don't know me!'

'Oh yes He does! He know everyone and He's everywhere!'

''Ow do you know?' Maisie was definitely getting the upper hand. The situation was rescued by the reappearance of the matron carrying a towel.

'Ah, there you are, you two. Are you ready now, Maisie?' She marched off purposefully, calling back to me, 'You can come too.'

19

How things had changed! In the old days, Maisie would have been dragged kicking and screaming to the bath.

I helped dry her hair with my own towel. The poor child was covered in scars, but looked completely different scrubbed and dressed in the winter uniform of pale blue jersey and navy gymslip.

There was no chapel in the grounds. Every Sunday the girls were distributed around the local churches for morning service. We looked forward to the long walks down country lanes, past fields and cottages. We were taken, crocodile fashion, on roundabout routes, perhaps to avoid unnecessary contact with the local population.

Most churches had emergency inter-denominational services and, in view of the number of girls, the sermons were simple and the stories of Jesus lovingly explained. Gone were the terrors and fears instilled by the patriarchal bellowings from the pulpit at the old Orphanage, causing rows of little children to shrink visibly. I wouldn't shrink! Daringly defying damnation this instant, I would sit up straight, never taking my eyes off the preacher, until his face would recede, becoming a mere speck in a dark void.

One day a number of girls, including myself, were inspected for lice, which were common. The mystery of eternal itching and scratching was solved. We had ring-worm! Our hair was cut short and lotions and potions were rubbed vigorously into our heads. For some this was enough, but for Maisie, another little girl and myself, the condition persisted. The matrons resorted to pulling hair out with tweezers, but the effort proved too much. It was frightfully painful and the shrieks and cries reduced everyone to a frazzle.

Accompanied by a matron, the three of us were taken to Canterbury Hospital. The carbolic smell reminded me of the old Orphanage. We were sent to the X-ray department. On the way, a man shuffled towards me. I looked up at him and recoiled in horror. His lower face, massively disfigured and strangely powdered, almost touched mine as we collided. I stifled a scream as he lurched past me, but not a word was said as we carried on through endless corridors.

A nurse with icy hands fixed my head with the aid of clamps into an awesome, silent X-ray machine. I couldn't imagine what they would do to me. I was filled with dread. The nurse disappeared behind a wall. Suddenly there was a thin whine from the great machine. My heart thundered, a dreadful panic rose within me and I struggled to free myself, but I was held fast. I let out a scream. The nurse released me.

'What was that for? Were you hurt? Well I never! What a fuss!'

I ran out of the room and away from the whining bogey in the X-ray contraption. It hadn't hurt at all and I felt a bit ashamed. We left the hospital wearing little cotton caps. They were rather nice, almost as good as a bandage, I thought.

That evening, back at the Orphanage, I began to feel restless. I thought the elastic was too tight and put my hands to my head. It was hot. Soon the three of us were vomiting and were put to bed.

Now I was struggling with the shuffling man from the hospital! I managed to wriggle from him, but he was chasing me through the stone corridors of the old Orphanage. In front of me I saw two forms. I tried to run to them, screaming for help, but I wasn't moving! With a supreme effort, my heart thumping, I reached them. Miss Frampton held out her large scissors. 'Child of the devil!' she shrieked. Miss Marriott clutched at me. Turning to run from them, I collided with the shuffling man. He grabbed me! His swollen, weeping, powdered sores were about to touch my face.

'Dor . . . roth . . . thy!' I yelled.

Dorothy held my hands, 'I'm here my little sister.'

With great relief, I saw Dorothy, with the light of the sun behind her. The net curtains swayed in the breeze.

Suddenly perceiving blank walls, I cried out. 'My people! Where are my people?' and fell into a fit of sobbing. Dorothy looked mystified. 'On the wall,' I pointed. 'My people have gone!'

After retching and vomiting I was asleep again.

It seemed an age before I felt better. Under my now bandaged head, my scalp had peeled and it was very sore. But healing finally produced a new, very shiny skin. Moving back to my own dormitory, I was relieved to find the couple seated beneath the tree once more decorating the walls.

Christmas came and went. My ninth birthday arrived in April. Still not a visible hair on my head. Ashamed of having no hair, I wondered if it would ever grow again. By now, the three of us hated the little white cloth caps. On the long walks, it seemed that people stared at us. Somewhere in the Bible, I'd read that a woman's hair is her crowning glory. The hymn, 'Will there be any stars, any stars in my crown . . .' would have my eyes brimming as I pictured myself looking ridiculous with a crown upon my bald head. This was an awful feeling. All the wallops and taunts in the world had never made me sad for longer than five minutes, but the feelings I was now experiencing were truly painful, so I flung them away together with the little white cap.

The first time I remembered any change in the day-to-day pattern of the year came with the school holidays in the summer. We were off to the seaside! Thrilled and excited, we piled into coaches and arrived in Broadstairs on a glorious day. It was the first time I had ever seen the sea. How beautiful it was, how expansive.

With some trepidation I approached the water, joining the other girls already splashing about the edges. I was astonished at the saltiness and coldness of the sea. It was then, with the hairs on my skin raised with the cold, that I found my hair was growing.

In a few weeks my head was covered in soft baby curls. Oh joy! Oh happiness!

The war seemed far away. Spurgeon's Orphanage, I learned, was on the fringe of Reigate in Surrey. Often at night the air-raid sirens would wail out the cry of enemy bombers overhead, but they always flew harmlessly on, presumably to London. Nevertheless we would be roused from our sleep, made to dress in haste and file silently through the grounds to the shelters. There was an atmosphere of magic as we swiftly shuffled through the leaves in the moonlight as if acting some play. A great sense of urgency hastened our steps towards the mounds, where the little ones would be passed down the ladders. We would lie head to tail, three on a bunk and fall fast asleep again, until the droning of the all-clear signal sent us sleepily on the trail back. Dazed with tiredness we would have to kneel in thanksgiving for our safety, then tumble into bed. Sometimes, in the morning, I had no recollection of the night's activities.

Then walks were curtailed and the seaside became out of bounds. Our last trip had been frustrated by soldiers erecting new signs. Great blocks of concrete and swirls of barbed wire against some impending invasion were strung across the beach-head. Silver barrage balloons were manned by laughing women soldiers, from the backs of trucks. Octagonal pill-boxes were being built and decorated with flint by old men with some artistry. For the first time I saw the real evidence of a threatened invasion. Sometimes I hoped that the Germans would come, then I'd pray fearfully for peace, lest I would be sucked into some abyss of terror.

A year passed and many avenues of interest opened up for me, as I learned more of the fundamentals of the world. I was, at last, settling down. My greatest interest was the Bible, and over the year I had endeavoured to read it from cover to cover. I perceived a glimpse of the great economy of the laws of nature, and viewed some of the harsher elements with disquiet.

Now aged ten, determined not to follow Dorothy's aspirations towards becoming a missionary, and even more determined never to be a domestic servant, I wondered about my future. I had developed a powerful, if vague, sense of my potential. It was while thinking upon these lines that I became aware of being addressed.

'Dreamer! Are you deaf or daft?' Maisie tugged at me. 'You're going 'ome! Your mum's here!'

I stared at her in disbelief.

Soon there was a ring of envious girls around me. 'Oh I wish I could come with you,' cried one little girl who burst into tears.

I sat in silent amazement, until Dorothy, tear-stained and looking thoroughly miserable, took me into the dining-room.

'Say you don't want to go! Say you want to stay here! Oh please!' she begged.

Visions of a pink and blue paradise, pretty china, bright lights and a proper home in a proper family flashed through my head. I shoved aside Dorothy's still pleading voice and accompanying tears.

'I do want to go! I want to go home!'

My body quickened as I reached out to that dream.

Although conditions had improved in the Orphanage, I felt not the slightest sorrow at the thought of leaving. Conscious that a chapter in my life had come to an end, I little realised, then, that there was to be no end to the influence these years would have on the rest of my life.

There was nothing to pack. I left nothing behind.

THREE

Stealing

Overwhelmed by the unfamiliar sights and sounds in the broad, busy streets, Dorothy and I, hand in hand, hugged the tall buildings, hardly aware of our mother and brother Anthony who marched on ahead. I was perturbed when the people we confronted showed us not a glimmer of recognition. Visitors to the Orphanage had shown such interest that it seemed odd to me that people passed us in the street with not so much as a glance in our direction.

We got off the bus at Baker Street and proceeded to Gloucester Place until we followed our mother down into what seemed a dark hovel. As we came directly into the living-room, Millicent was bending over the fireplace attempting to light the fire. She looked unkempt in a dirty pink dressing-gown and her hair, long and lanky, was stuck to her face. She was very pale and had grown quite tall. She'd been living at home for two years.

'Didn't I tell you to have that lit early, you slut.'

Mother pushed Millicent away and, kneeling, busied herself with the fire while Dorothy and I exchanged anxious glances.

We stood silently and gazed around the room in amazement at the filth and disorder; the table littered with knives in pots, and newspapers for a table cloth, heaps of clothes on the too-few chairs, the mantelpiece cluttered with make-up, papers and brass polishing equipment; and the brass ornaments which seemed to be everywhere.

'Put the kettle on, then,' Mother said to Millicent who moved about slowly, not acknowledging our presence.

'Now my darlings, I've been very ill.' My mother's voice was suddenly tremulous. 'We were to have cleared all this up,' she said, looking at the retreating spectre of Millicent. 'You'll see, we're going to be happy together. I couldn't bear to be parted from my little ones any longer.'

There was an awkward silence. There seemed to be nothing to say. Then Mother took a cigarette and lit it hastily. I watched her, fascinated and astonished. I'd seen a soldier doing this once when on a walk, but the matron quickly ordered us away.

'I had meant to give this up,' Mother said apologetically. 'I've not had one since I picked you three up. It's made my nerves bad . . . I've been lying in bed for days . . . Millicent was to tidy up. She's been under a strain, poor darling . . . I lost my temper with her, didn't I? It was too bad of me!' As she spoke, she was quickly clearing the table.

Then, giving a brilliant smile, she went to take Dorothy's hand, but Dorothy drew it away.

I quickly put my hand in hers deeply sorry for her, loving her, liking the smell and swirl of the smoke, the beautiful modulated tones of her voice, and her small, pretty hands with their long nails. She wore no make-up, there was no slash of red. I liked the proud tilt of her head and her dark, soft eyes.

She dropped my hand and tried to pull Dorothy to her. 'Come my precious, come to Mummy!' but Dorothy went rigid, with a look of distaste. Mother turned away and I saw the pain in her eyes.

'Well my chickens, supper and to bed?' she said cheerfully.

We were all tired out.

'Dorothy!' called Millicent. 'You're here with me; don't touch anything of mine!'

Dorothy squeezed my hand. 'I told you!' she whispered.

'Come on, you two!' Mother called. 'It's not much, but it's home.' Anthony and I followed her into a tiny back room with only one bed.

Anthony recoiled. 'I can't sleep in here!' he cried.

'Oh. Come on, you're the man around here now. Now, now. No tears.' With gentle, derisive tones, Mother coaxed him through the door. I quickly followed.

He fought back the tears, took off his short trousers, jacket and shirt and got into the bed with an air of absolute dejection. He lay close to the wall. I slipped in next to him. I made a great effort not to touch him. The bed was damp and smelled musty with no sheets under the coarse, itchy blankets. I mused on the thought of Mother calling Anthony the man of the house, when in fact he was a great baby. Listening to his sobs, and not daring to intrude into his misery, I fell asleep.

The sounds of clattering crockery woke me. Anthony had already risen, so I stretched myself and slipped on my dress, eager to see what the day held for me.

Dorothy and Anthony were busy cleaning and scrubbing. Mother was nowhere to be seen.

'There,' said Dorothy thrusting a none-too-clean towel at me with a smile. 'Have a good wash and don't forget your neck. We'll have breakfast and a talk before Mother gets back.'

Millicent was in the tiny bathroom idly slopping clothing up and down over the top of the dirty water that filled the bath. 'You can do this after you've eaten.'

Her speech was as slow as her movements. She seemed enormously tired. A little nervous of her, I held out my grubby towel to indicate my wish to use the sink. She lurched past me. I washed sparingly and joined the others in the living-room.

We sat down to a clean table and had lashings of home-made jam (we'd had a scrape of jam only on Sundays at the

Orphanage) on thick-sawn bread. We ate off lovely cream plates with a border of orange fruit round the edges. We used cups with saucers and drank tea with as much sugar as one could wish for. Anthony had brightened up and the three of us were chatting happily when Millicent joined us at the table. I offered to give up my seat (there were only three chairs), but Dorothy made Anthony get up and sit on a wooden box too low for him. I thought that Millicent should have sat on it.

'What do you do with yourself all day?' Dorothy addressed Millicent, eyeing her lovely, long, almost black hair as yet uncombed.

'For one thing, it's none of your business,' she said trying to summon up enough energy to sound emphatic, 'and for another . . .' but she trailed off. We all looked at her intently. There was something odd about her. She was like a witch. The whites of her eyes were yellow. Bright yellow!

Dorothy moved around the table, pushed aside the wild hair and placed a hand on her forehead.

'You don't look well, Millicent.'

'Leave me, I'm just tired.'

But Dorothy persisted. 'Your eyes are a funny colour, that's not right. Come, I think you must go to bed.'

Millicent visibly pleased with the suggestion, followed Dorothy into their bedroom, with me traipsing after them. 'Make the bed,' I was ordered while Dorothy sat Millicent on a low chest and proceeded to take the tangles out of her hair.

'Don't!' cried Millicent. But Dorothy had taken charge of the situation and soon had her elder sister washed and tidied and into bed.

Dorothy then directed Anthony and me into the bathroom to wash out the great quantity of laundry still in the bath. 'Change the water!' she sang out.

We began to have great fun inspecting the various peculiar garments. There was a Chinese dressing-gown with a yellow

dragon on the back, lots of camiknickers, dirndl skirts and pais-
ley-patterned oddments. A body-length corset was hanging on
the line over the bath; this we tried on amid hoots of laughter,
although neither of us knew the purpose of the lace cups with
various dangling straps. Anthony had no idea how to wash
clothes and I delighted in showing off my skill as we two
became friends. Anthony was a sweet, gentle lad, not at all like
the boys I had heard described by older girls at the Orphanage.

'Yoo-hOO!' We heard Mother call outside as she came down
the steps. She'd got bundles, bags and bulging paper parcels.
The three of us rushed to take her load and she laughed as we
all pushed through the door. Then, seeing the sitting-room all
neat she cried, 'My angels! My good children! My darlings!' Her
voice sounded like a sweet bell. I felt myself smiling happily at
the realisation that these pretty words included me.

Mother plomped herself on a chair. 'Put the kettle on, then.'
She was addressing Dorothy, who nervously approached the
gas stove.

'I don't know how to work this,' she said. 'I put the kettle on
the fire this morning.'

'On the fire!' Mother's tones were derisory. Dorothy backed
away from her. I saw a glint of anger in Mother's eyes.

'Come on, little four eyes! Come, I'll teach Miss Uppity how
to use a common-or-garden gas stove.' Dorothy just stood there.
'Oh, come on. I didn't mean to upset you, love.'

Dorothy squinted behind her thick lenses. Her large, almost
violet, blue eyes, looked small behind her glasses. She had a
habit of taking her spectacles off and fiercely rubbing her face;
she was doing this now. Mother grasped her hand, causing her
to drop her glasses. Dorothy gave her a look of revulsion which
induced a sharp slap. The previously happy atmosphere
degenerated into misery.

I earnestly watched the lighting of the fearsome gas stove as

Mother made the tea. (Later Anthony and I, when left alone, lit it again and again.)

'Where did Millicent go?'

'She's in bed. Her eyes are all yellow!' I offered, eager to please, to placate, as I gently rested my hand on her arm. Anthony stood behind Dorothy, both of them looking forlorn.

'We've done all the washing, me and Anthony!' But she shook me off and went to see Millicent.

She hurried back with a look of alarm. 'I'm taking Millicent to the hospital. I got some clothes from the Church Army, you can sort out what's best for you. No. I think you'd better come with me, Dorothy.'

Rushing to the mirror over the mantelpiece, she plastered her face with creams and powders, carelessly applying lipstick.

'Dorothy, get your sister dressed. I don't know how I'm going to cope with you all.'

Millicent looked dazed and was almost pushed up the steps as they left. 'Mind you two behave!' Mother called to us. 'And don't go out and don't answer the door if anyone knocks!'

Left to ourselves, we set out to explore the flat. There was a large collection of articulated brass ornaments, some with little levers, all brightly polished, all different. There was a camel; if you pressed the back of its neck a tented sedan chair arose from its back.

As we poked around, looking in drawers and cupboards, we discussed our ages. Millicent was fifteen, Dorothy fourteen, Anthony twelve-and-a-half and I was ten. Dorothy had made us say prayers at breakfast and we wondered if it really worked and whether Dorothy really would become a missionary. Anthony said he'd like to be a farmer, or join the navy and see the world. I said I didn't know what I wanted to be. 'Magnificent!' is what I thought.

We talked and had a lot of fun just mucking about and the day went like the wind. It became nearly dark and Anthony decided to light a fire. Great flames leapt up in the grate. With an umbrella he retrieved sheets of newspaper that had now been sucked up the chimney. The umbrella was now alight. Just then Mother arrived. We hadn't heard her come in. She rushed over and pulled Anthony so hard that he fell flat on his back. Dorothy ran to him. I jumped out of reach.

'My God! You nearly set the place on fire!' Mother cried, as she put out the flames that had been licking the mantelpiece.

'I don't know why I picked you lot up,' she sighed regretfully as she sat down, smoothing out the remains of her silk dressing-gown with which she'd smothered the flames.

Anthony disappeared with Dorothy.

I was eager to console Mother. 'We're sorry, it was so pretty. We were just making the place warm for you!'

She burst out laughing. 'You'll be the death of me! Come help me with the dinner. We'll have to do without Millicent for a while, she has jaundice, but she'll be all right. Why haven't you put the shopping away?'

'Didn't know whether to open your bags,' I replied. I wouldn't have dared to touch one of the matron's bags in the Orphanage.

'Well! There's nothing in those to bite you. Come on, have a look.'

There were two tins of pilchards, spices and vegetables, some of which I had never seen before, rice and a bag of sweets. The last caused a cry of delight.

That evening we had the most marvellous curry. The fire forgotten, we listened to wonderful stories of India. How she'd been brought up like a queen, with a house and servants all to herself, with private tutors, and jewels and even a pony! How she suffered when her father died, leaving her almost no money; and she'd had to sell everything and come to Europe by herself to start a new life. That night I fell asleep dreaming of pearls, princesses and being waited on hand and foot.

*

Soon Anthony and I went out on our own. Although there had been no air raids since we arrived in London, we saw signs of previous devastating bombings. We wandered further and further every day, exploring and taking in unfamiliar scenes.

We'd copy other children skipping and chanting behind American soldiers. 'Got any gum, chum?' Kindly hand-outs by these genial giants provided many hours of urgent chewing.

It was now evident, even to me, that there was something wrong with Mother. When she was happy the sun came out, but often she would suddenly change and the least thing made her fearfully angry. She would lie in bed for days. She couldn't be bothered to provide food but would send Dorothy out for cigarettes. Dorothy would plead not to be asked to go out.

One day, I was chasing Anthony through a vegetable market. As I ran, I grabbed at the fruit, scattering some in the process. The shouts from the stall-holders spurred me on as I raced wildly, breathlessly depositing my haul into Anthony's out-stretched arms.

Just two apples, yet Anthony's face fell. 'That's stealing!' he cried. 'You stole them!'

'Oh Anthony! It's just fun,' I remonstrated. 'I'm hungry.' I placed my arm on his, but he shook it off. I felt a lump in my throat. 'Oh Anthony please, don't be a pig!' I cried almost bursting into tears.

'Oh, come on.' He cast an anxious glance towards the market, took the apples from me and bit into the biggest one, offering me the other as we raced away from the scene.

That was the beginning.

As we explored the big stores, playfully saying, 'I'll have that, and I'll have that. Oh well, all right then, you can have that . . .', somehow we would end up in the grocers' department. I would deftly snatch and secrete items about my person. At first

Anthony wasn't aware that I had done so. He accepted his share grudgingly, his hunger finally overcoming his well-formed principles.

Eventually, driven by a frightful guilt, he told Dorothy.

Dorothy, horrified, urged me to think on the commandment: *Thou Shalt Not Steal*! She was at a loss to know quite how to deal with this new problem. 'I'll get a job and earn some money and you won't be hungry,' she said, and begged me never to steal again. Needing Dorothy's approval, I vowed I never would. 'I won't! Really I won't, Dorothy!' And I meant it.

I read the ten commandments over; actually, I knew them all by heart. While I could not quite understand them, I felt a certain umbrage over some of the wording. 'Thou shalt not covet thy neighbour's house. Thou shalt not covet thy neighbour's wife, nor his manservant, nor his maidservant, nor his ox, nor his ass, nor anything that is thy neighbour's.' Well! I thought, who's God talking to? Dorothy? Me, Marian Hughes? Were all women lumped together with the house, servants and domestic animals? Could I have a wife? It dawned on me that most of what was written in my beloved Bible was addressed to men.

'What a cheek!' I said to Dorothy as I tried to voice these feelings. She wouldn't listen, saying only that I had a head full of nonsense and that sometimes she feared for my future. Anthony agreed with her, trusting Dorothy's command of the subject, and I was left with a sense of isolation. Yet it seemed that only I read the Bible constantly.

There were books in the family. I ploughed through all of Dickens, which I loved; was terrified by the Brothers Grimm, but found their fearful tales compulsive; adored the *Arabian Nights*. Feeling a bit of an outcast at home, I revelled in almost any book I could lay my hands on.

And I did steal again.

FOUR

War

Millicent arrived after a long stay at the hospital. With her was a woman in a green uniform.

At first refusing her entry, Mother allowed the stranger inside after she explained that Millicent might require extra things for the convalescence home. The lady politely declined a cup of tea. I noticed her eyes quickly taking in all around her, and her expression became severe as she sniffed the air in obvious distaste. I sided with Mother in her rebuff of this woman who dared stiffen in disapproval.

Millicent, rounder and rosy-cheeked, smiled and kissed me and Anthony, as we followed her into her bedroom. While Mother was busy with the lady, Millicent whispered that she'd soon be much better and would take us away from all this. She seemed hesitant with Dorothy, not being able to make out this grave girl who had adopted an air of taking care of all of us.

'You must leave home, Dorothy,' she said earnestly. 'Get a job in service. At least you'll get properly fed.'

Dorothy was indignant. 'I'm going to be a missionary. I've already applied to train as a nurse. I said I was older.'

'Do you think they believed you?' I said. Dorothy looked so fragile.

All three of us had become very thin, and Dorothy and I had sores breaking out at the corners of our mouths.

*

For the past few months Mother had spent most of the time sitting cross-legged on her bed writing and staring into space, a large ash-tray overflowing next to her. I would empty it and bring her cups of tea. Often she would be asleep most of the day and would potter about at night, occasionally going out in the evening. Frequently she was unapproachable. For days on end we would hardly see her. But brief moments of animation and the cooking of wonderful meals endeared her to me. I loved her tales of India and her travels around Europe. Her humour had me rolling about with laughter. Sometimes she would sing softly and beautifully in her room, and I would stand outside straining to hear.

Dorothy now had a job of sorts somewhere. She seemed a strangely strong, yet pathetic, little creature who struggled in the half light of the morning making her marmite sandwiches stealthily so as not to wake Mother, who now seemed to go into an uncontrollable rage over the least little thing.

It was evident that The Mother of The Letters had been just a dream. She was less and less able to cope with the three of us, and we no longer made an effort to keep the place clean and tidy. There was very little food, and Dorothy made sure that Anthony got most of what there was. With no money for gas and electric meters, we often went to bed early, grindingly hungry, and awoke in the same state.

It was on such a morning, after Dorothy had left for her long walk to work, that another lady came to the door. Hunger had driven me to be up in the early light to pick over possible remains of food in corners missed in yesterday's search at dusk. Forgetting for the moment the strict instructions that positively no one was allowed entry, I let her in.

'I've come to tell your mother that Millicent is settling down nicely,' she said as she eased through the door. 'Are you her sister?'

'I'm the youngest, my other sister's at work,' I said hesitantly.

'Is your mother at home?' the lady asked brightly.

'She's still asleep.' I suddenly felt anxious. 'I don't like to wake her.'

'There's no hurry. Suppose we chat for a while?'

'Well, don't make a noise then.' Panic seized me. 'I mean, I don't think she'll like it . . . letting you in and . . .'

'It's all right, my dear. I just want a little talk.' She was calm and smiling. 'How old are you, Marian? You are Marian, aren't you?'

'Yes, and I'm nearly eleven,' I answered. Then, 'How do you know my name?'

'Millicent told us all about you. She said you're a bright little thing.' The lady smiled warmly, and I smiled shyly back at her.

The conversation seemed idle chat. No, I didn't go to school. No, I didn't want to go. No, I didn't want to leave my mother. Yes, I was hungry. No, we'd no money to put in the meter at present. Yes, I'd had a bath, last week, I thought. No, we never went to the shelters. No, I wasn't scared of the air raids. No, I wasn't cold.

Suddenly Mother burst into the room.

'How dare you!' she yelled. 'How did you get in here?'

I ran into the bathroom.

After some shouting and screaming, the nice lady was gone. The next thing, Mother was struggling with the handle of the bathroom door and yelling at me. 'I'll teach you to tell everyone our business, you little guttersnipe!' Inside, I pushed the door with all my might. She shrieked even louder, 'I'll thrash the living daylights out of you!'

Finally the door burst open.

Mother came at me, picking up a wooden-backed brush, and proceeded to lash out at me with savagery. I made myself as small as I could and tried to protect my head with my arms.

Then Anthony was screaming, holding Mother around her waist, and trying to drag her away from me. She turned and punched him in the stomach. He stood against the door fighting to breathe. Abruptly Mother returned to her senses and helped him.

I crawled into bed and stayed there until the evening waiting for Dorothy.

Dorothy eased me into the living-room. There was no light bulb in the bedroom. I wasn't trusted with the black-out. Anthony didn't mind, for the darkness gave him privacy. Seating me on a chair, Dorothy bathed my cuts which were fairly superficial, but the bruising was black and ugly.

Just then, Mother returned. She looked fantastic – so elegant and everything new. She had bags and bags of food, chocolate and niceties such as I had never seen. Clothes for Anthony, right down to underwear, and all with a Harrods label. All this she tipped out on to the table, not looking at the three of us who stared in amazement.

'There, my loves, things are looking up,' she trilled.

We fell upon the bounty. Cold cooked chicken, ham, a bottle of curried eggs, cake and many other agreeable delicacies.

The taxi-driver was standing in the doorway, forgotten, with an expression of amazement directed at the trio of ragamuffins in the dingy room full of damp, grey washing and general clutter on every surface. He put more bags on the floor.

'Ah, there you are. Here!' She took out a wad of notes from her new handbag, gave him too much, and he departed.

Looking at Mother, I thought how stunning she was, even with the lipstick.

Now she came almost shyly towards me, and was lifting my chin and gazing earnestly into my eyes. 'I'm sorry, darling, will you ever forgive me?'

Her look was so distressed that I wanted this extravagant atmosphere to remain forever.

'Oh, it's all right, Mummy. It doesn't hurt much at all!'

She gently boxed my nose. 'That's the first time you've called me Mummy!' She smiled, I thought a little sadly.

She included the others as she called, 'Let's eat!'

Dorothy had been busy washing the dishes in cold water and had directed Anthony to the clearing of a sideboard so as to remove the heap on the table. Soon we were merrily chatting and satisfying our hunger.

When we asked where it all came from, Mother pursed her lips, placing her forefinger to them, and smilingly whispered, 'Shush!'

'We're moving!' she announced. 'We're threatened with the bailiffs and anyway that nosy woman is up to something. By the way you two will have to go to school.' Anthony and I looked at each other in dismay. We hated the idea. 'It's no good looking like that. You'll have to go and that's that.'

'What about my job?' demanded Dorothy. 'I have to keep my job.'

'Oh, you can keep your job, you won't have to walk so far. We'll leave tomorrow night.'

'Tomorrow *night*!' echoed Dorothy. 'That's not possible! Why must we go at night?'

Mother raised her hands. 'Because, my lady, we don't wish to be seen. We're doing what's called a moonlight flit!'

'But you have some money!' Dorothy pleaded.

'Yes, and we're going to need every penny of it if we're not to live like this for the rest of our lives!'

'Where *did* the money come from?'

I wished Dorothy'd shut up.

'For God's sake!' snapped Mother, with exasperation in her voice. Dorothy had removed her glasses and was rubbing her face. 'Stop doing that! Are you sure you need those?'

'I can't see without them,' said Dorothy very quietly.

'You look like a cripple in them!'

'Shall Anthony try on these lovely clothes?' I cried. By now

I had realised that Mother's rages were often preceded by malicious observations.

'I'm not having those clothes made filthy!'

Mother's movements were jerky.

'Mummy you do look tired, buying us all these lovely things. Shall I make you a cup of tea?'

I was bent on pacification. It wasn't wholly that, though. Up till today, none of us had called her anything; now twice I'd called her 'Mummy', and from now on I always would. I desperately wished Dorothy would love her. It seemed that whenever Mother talked to the three of us, she was always addressing Dorothy. But Dorothy didn't warm to her. Indeed, she seemed almost to hate her. Mother, continually repulsed, would take to her bed, containing her grief, or roar with the pain of it, creating terror among us. Dorothy seemed to see her own mother as a threat to her existence. I pitied both of them.

Mummy went to bed and I brought her tea and dared to kiss her cheek.

Before dawn, we packed everything, and in each case or bundle we put three or four brass ornaments; there didn't seem to be very much else. Mummy was full of energy and her efficiency was a joy to behold.

The moonlight flit was to be one of many. I thoroughly enjoyed these escapades, as I entered into the spirit of the adventure. They were loathed equally by Dorothy, who regarded them as a shameful experience. Our family never paid any rent. A lot of property was available as many people had fled to the country to escape the bombing. Often a summons, never accepted, precipitated our moves.

I was now eleven years old.

Still not at school, Anthony and I roamed the streets from morning until night. We suffered little from hunger. What I stole I shared with Anthony. Mars was our favourite, for sweets were not yet rationed.

The two of us found a new pursuit. The cinema! I loved the wonder of the movies, adored being transported to the jungle by Tarzan films, elated by the beat of the drum, the dancing of the natives, and terrified by the witch doctors. Revelling in the great dramas I fell in love for the first time – with Charles Laughton. His passionate, powerful portrayal of the frail human condition, his almost arrogant humility, dignity and humorous clowning. . . . Mummy roared with laughter when I confessed this great love.

Then there was bold, brash Hollywood. Terrible films which were sat through for the sake of jazz. Jazz blotted out everything, set my body moving and lifted my spirits. Jazz was surely the music for heaven on earth.

One of the cinemas we visited was the Blue Hall in the Edgware Road. I would climb through the ladies' lavatory window, slither on my belly, open an exit door for Anthony, and, together in like manner, we'd creep through the aisles, to surface on either side of an unfortunate couple, adopting an air of belonging to them.

Another was the Roxy. We didn't care for foreign films, but I loved the older, slick American comedies often portraying powerfully intelligent and confident heroines who melted into the arms of an agreeable lover.

We were now very conscious of the war, which had taken on a new significance. There had been a lull in the frequency of the raids, but now suddenly sirens seemed to sound almost every night. We hadn't ever been to the shelters; Mummy vowed she never would. Our windows, like everyone's, had strips of paper pasted cross-wise all over them, and at dusk we would have to draw black-out curtains. When Anthony and I pulled them aside to watch the searchlights, we heard the sharp retort, 'Put that light out!' It was a phrase we were to hear many times. We sometimes heard bombs falling with a tremendous wallop, but mostly they were in the distance. Dorothy was terrified, but Anthony and I were not at all afraid – for now.

The war became part of our adventure playground. The two of us would wander about with morbid curiosity after an air raid, hoping to see somebody dead. One day we were watching the demolition of an unsafe building. A crane swung over us, lifting an iron bedstead, and the body of a young soldier rolled off and fell at our feet. His face, covered in fine dust, looked like that of a well-fed child asleep.

We ran away and never spoke of it.

Things got worse, and eventually we did go to the shelters. In one air raid, Dorothy and Anthony had just run off (for some reason I stayed behind), when a huge blast blew out our windows. Part of the ceiling came down on Mummy. For a moment she just sat there, with blood slowly oozing from her head. I watched in horror, not daring to move. Suddenly she stood up, clenching her fists, and delivering fearsome curses to Hitler! Her voice screamed above my fright; her eyes dilated and her energy was awesome. I found her more terrifying than the bomb.

We moved out. And moved again. Nineteen-forty-two brought us to Westbourne Grove Terrace, off Westbourne Grove. On one corner was the Timpo toy factory where they smelted lead for toys. Greatly daring, Anthony would leap from our roof to the roof of the factory, to steal brand-new boxed toys, which he and I would sell to passers-by, who believed they were unwanted Christmas presents. Almost opposite was Pritchard's which sold bread and cakes, and became the unwitting and frequent suppliers of wholesome nutrients. The other corner housed a bank, where tight-lipped people with rigid faces came and went. Further up the street, in Westbourne Grove, was a window behind which people with large magnifying glasses did invisible mending to drab clothes. I would grimace at their hostility towards my freedom as I watched their expressions distort through the large lenses, until they rose in impotent fury. Then there was the Roxy cinema almost in our street too.

The top-floor flat was light and airy. Below was an A.R.P. station, where old men's guffaws were often heard. There were always comings and goings on the stairs. At night the old chaps would come up to the top of the stairs to the attic and then on to the roof, carrying their binoculars. Anthony and I would join them among the sandbags, watching the searchlights, the fires and the dogfights overhead. They were brave, stubble-chinned, red-eyed old men, who never seemed to sleep. Mummy thought them a nuisance. She didn't mind the sounds of the air raids, but couldn't stand the noise of the wardens and forbade us to have contact with them.

We were sent to school, after the visit of a busy-body, who had bolted unceremoniously out of the flat. We had all laughed at her exit and Mummy's tirade down the stairs as she retreated in terror.

'Hoity toity old bag!' I had yelled after her, and then I'd felt sorry that I'd done so.

Now I found myself seated in what seemed to be a hall of ignorance, Cosway Street Elementary School. On the very first day, I had to hold out my hand to the headmaster to receive strokes from the cane, because I'd stood on a pile of coke. I'd given him my direct look of disdain, and hadn't flinched, thus inviting another and another whack. A rage rose within me. I seized the cane and lashed out. Then, trying desperately but unsuccessfully to break it over my knee, I flung it at him and ran out of the school.

Thus that half day ended my formal education forever.

Anthony stayed on miserably. He was clearly unhappy and I persuaded him to join me on the streets.

We pretended to Mummy that we were still at school. Sometimes she even gave us dinner money. This we would use on the buses and trying out the underground railways where we saw hundreds of people bringing their bedding for the night's sleep on the platforms. In the early morning the trains were full of people with bundles, but later in the day no sight of the great encampment was evident.

The bombing worsened. From our roof one night, Anthony and I watched the school (we were quite sure it was the school) burning. We roared and cheered with delight, egged on by the four old wardens who had given up trying to make us go to the shelters.

Then, while Anthony and I were larking about with a pair of binoculars, a great batch of incendiary bombs landed upon our roof. The two of us flattened ourselves against the chimney stack.

'Jesus! Jesus Christ! Get those kids down . . .' But before the old man could continue, smoke and an ominous hissing erupted from one of the cylinders.

Time stood still for what must have been an instant.

Then there was a sudden rush, a fever of action, as the wardens picked up the bombs with their bare hands and threw them, or kicked them with their feet, into the street below.

One, Arthur, my dearest, was suddenly engulfed in white-hot, magnesium-like flames.

Anthony rushed over to him, taking off his jacket as he did so, and swung it about in a vain, but brave attempt to beat out the flames, as another and yet another bomb created an inferno.

'Bloody hell! *Bloody, bloody hell!*' screamed Anthony and threw his burning jacket down. He saw, and I knew, as I stood petrified watching the flurry of activity, that our friend was dying.

43

Then it was all over.

The three remaining wardens, themselves injured, were kneeling over the still-smoking body.

One of them cradled the lifeless form, patting out the smoking parts of his clothing, as he hugged and rocked old Arthur to him.

Anthony and I both wept.

In the morning we saw burns on the road where the heroes had thrown and kicked the bombs.

FIVE

Remanded

It was summer, but it rained and rained. Dorothy was home with a head cold. Anthony and I lay around reading or just gazing at the rain out of the window. Mummy had unexpectedly dressed and gone out, and Dorothy was kneeling on the floor, going through the old tin hat box containing our mother's incessant writings.

'This is all in Latin,' she sang out authoritatively. 'And here's some, I think it's German. I can't read it.'

Anthony and I squatted either side of Dorothy.

'German?' he queried and pored excitedly over the neat writing. 'Wow! She could spy on the Nazis when they invade.'

'Oh Dorothy you are so clever. How do you know all this?' I cried.

'Dorothy knows everything,' Anthony said with conviction. His face lit with proud admiration as he gazed adoringly upon his sister. He stretched himself on the floor and looked up at the ceiling. 'Want to know anything? Ask Dorothy.'

'Mummy was very, very clever,' she sighed. 'I take after her, in some things. The good things, I hope.'

Suddenly she cried out and burst into tears.

Anthony and I were at her side. She held up a cutting from the *News of the World*. It contained an account of our father's suicide. We read the newspaper story together. James Hughes had leapt off Hungerford Bridge, and drowned himself in the Thames. He had been unable to find work and could no longer support his wife and four children. He had been living with his family in one room in the road opposite the gasworks, but had been given notice to quit because he could not pay the rent.

I had never really given him much thought. I'd merely decided that he'd inadvertently popped out of my life soon after it had begun. Immediately, the wicked thought occurred to me that I should say 'plopped'! Then, with an odd feeling of guilt, I felt sorry for his poor starving little children.

'Suicide does mean he killed himself, doesn't it?' I said, not quite understanding Dorothy's consternation.

Anthony, who had turned away from us, swung around revealing his tears. 'Why did he do that?'

I'd never actually seen Anthony cry. The first night home from the Orphanage, he had lain quietly sobbing for the day's indignities, but I hadn't seen the spread of anguish that engulfed him now. Without quite knowing why, I joined in the tears and the three of us clung together.

'I hate him! I hate him!' Anthony howled, stabbing the air with his fists.

'Perhaps he didn't mean to. Perhaps he couldn't swim,' I said helpfully. I was holding the newspaper cutting, sitting on the floor amongst the scattered papers next to the open tin box.

Then I saw Mummy standing in the doorway, taking it all in.

She leapt upon us, punching all three of us. She snatched at Dorothy's glasses and seemed to grind them in her hands. Suddenly the room was in a whirl.

'You four-eyed bloody little bitch!' she screamed as she lashed out ferociously at Dorothy. 'I'll teach you! You'll never touch my things again!'

Like an arrow, I shot out of the flat and part-way down the stairs, breathlessly listening to the repeated thuds and yells.

I banged on the wardens' door. Four of the old men rushed

46

up the stairs, only to be thrown back by the mad strength her fury gave her.

As they came down sheepishly, I dived into their flat and hid behind a steel desk, shivering with terror.

'Jesus Christ! Them kids!' said one hoarsely. 'Get on the phone. Get the police in.'

I heard him begin to dial and popped out of my hiding place, surprising a white-faced old chap who put out his hand as if to detain me. I streaked out of the open door.

'Come back, Missie. You'll be safe here, with us old codgers,' he stage-whispered to me as I clung half-way down the next flight of stairs holding on to the banister rail and looking up at him.

I shook my head and took off slowly down to the front door.

Moments later three policemen arrived. Without noticing my presence, they passed by me. I listened intently as they stopped and consulted the wardens, then heard their determined stomping on the steps up to our flat. I heard again the rage of my mother, and now the shouts of the policemen. So violent was she that they were no match for her. They seemed almost to tumble back down the stairs. Their pace slackened as they came into view, avoiding shamefacedly the wardens' flat.

'That woman's crazy, for God's sake,' cried one. A tirade followed them. 'I know people in the right places,' yelled my mother.

'Should be certified!' exclaimed another.

'Family dispute,' said the older policeman. 'Can't get mixed up. Tough on the kids, though.' Yet he seemed to startle and glance directly at me as he passed out into the street.

I hung around inside the front door, listening fearfully and feeling very anxious. Finally it grew quiet. I waited some more and eventually, with some trepidation, I mounted the stairs.

As I reached the top Mummy suddenly pounced on me.

I screamed in terror as I evaded her grasp, hurtled down the stairs and out into the street, not listening to the mad fury of the threats that followed me.

I was desperate. I couldn't ever go home again. Mummy didn't love me; anyway she was mad. My father had killed himself; so he didn't love me either. Dorothy knew I was a thief. Anthony always took Dorothy's side. I didn't love me much. I was skinny, spotty, and wore tatty shoes. Sod 'em all! I thought. Damn God! Damn Jesus! Stinking sod 'em all!

I wandered the streets getting absolutely drenched, until darkness fell. I remembered the underground station where people slept. Sure enough, it seemed that at least a hundred people were preparing to spend the night. I weaved through the throng, some singing as they cheerfully folded blankets, and finally squatted next to a fat woman with a bunch of children.

'What's the matter, love, lost your folks?'

Grasping that idea, feeling truly that it was so, I tearfully replied: 'I've looked all over the place! I think they went somewhere else.'

She wiped my eyes with a well-used handkerchief and gave me a delicious sandwich. She put her enormous arm around me and snuggled my dampness close to her.

I awoke early in the morning, still nestled in her arm, the fat woman still asleep.

I crept away. Shivering, I sought the sunny side of the street. For sure, I've caught Dorothy's cold, I thought. Then, 'Must have a wash!' I muttered aloud as I surveyed my hands. I entered Whiteley's department store through the food-hall, and was soon helping myself.

'Got you! Caught you red-handed!'

A large hand belonging to a tall angular store assistant had grabbed me by the back of my clothes. I froze, then struggled wildly, but all my thrashing about was to no avail.

'She's a filthy little thing and I swear she tried to bite me! So watch out!' The lady wiped her hands on her hips as she placed me on a chair.

Oh God! I want to go home, I thought. I felt my eyes watering. Don't cry, for God's sake, don't cry, I said to myself. Lifting my head, I tried to manage my haughty stare, but my nose started to run, and I grudgingly took the proffered handkerchief.

'What's your name child?'

'Maisie Stocks!' I answered, quick as a whistle.

'And where do you live?'

'Nowhere!'

I was offered a glass of water. The glass was so purely translucent, I almost gasped as I was oddly transported momentarily on to some other plane of consciousness with this vision of startling beauty.

The lady shook my shoulder. 'Come on, love, where have you come from?' Her voice was kind. 'We can't keep you here.'

'I'm sorry I took the things. Can I go now?'

'Where will you go?'

'Straight home, and I won't take anything again, really I won't!'

'All right then, but tell us first where "home" is?'

I made a bolt for the door.

Again I was grasped by my clothing and held until the police arrived. Then I was bundled into a car with plain-clothed policewomen either side of me and shortly arrived at Paddington Police Station. There, more questions and another ride, like a dream, to a remand centre somewhere in Hammersmith, where I was put to bed and glad of it.

'Hey! What you 'ere for?'

I was nudged awake by two girls kneeling at my bed. Just for a moment, I thought I was back in the old Orphanage.

'I ran away!' I volunteered.

'Where you run from?'

'From home.'

'Is that all? You'll get "Care an' Protection". They'll just send you back.'

Staring into space I remembered miserably that I couldn't go back. Besides, I was a thief. I hadn't told the girls that.

'Don't worry.' One of them patted me cheerfully. 'Just do what they tell you. You'll be all right.'

The sound of a key turning sent the girls scattering back to their beds.

'Rise and shine, for the light has come and the glory of the Lord is upon us.' This explosion came from a tiny Scots woman. Ten or so girls jumped out of bed, grabbed their towels and toothbrushes and stood in a row. I quickly joined them.

'Not you. You have a temperature.' She pointed to my bed.

'I'm all right, Miss,' I called, eager to explore the new day.

'Back into bed with you.' She watched my hesitation. 'At once!'

I sprang back into bed. Off they went, chatting away. They'd not have been allowed to make that din at the Orphanage, I mused. Soon the girls were back again, noisily dressing in neat blue gingham and cardigans.

'Order! Order!'

They raced to form a queue for the door, then they were gone.

Alone, I shot out of bed and looked out of the window. Down below there was a small playground with painted circles on the tarmac. A high brick wall against which leaned a low brick building. I heard the clatter of the kitchens somewhere below and sniffed hungrily at the aroma of bacon.

'Into bed!' a voice barked, and I leapt in. 'Nothing much wrong with you, my girl.'

'No. I feel all right,' I said to the Scottish matron.

'Well, you're not all right until the doctor says you are.' She thrust forward a tray. My disappointment showed. 'Light breakfast, you're on light food.'

Wolfing down the toast and tea, I fished in my locker for my clothes, but there weren't any. Unable to lie still, I sprang from bed to bed with great daring, a favourite game from the old days. I remembered the glory of forty girls prancing and plunging in long white nighties, hair flying, from bed to bed, creating such an air of elation and energy. It had been worth all the subsequent stillness forced upon us, standing for hours, in punishment rows.

'What do you think you're doing?' The Scots lady had returned. I streaked into bed. 'You'd better lie quiet, you'll be seeing the doctor soon.'

'Make beds!' she called to the girls, who had trooped in after her.

Watching them, I saw most of the girls didn't know how to. They're an awful mess, I thought. But the matron didn't seem to notice. Soon they were off again. A big girl brought me a bowl of water to wash in. I remembered my dirty hands, now surprisingly almost clean. I couldn't remember having had a bath.

It seemed an age until I found myself traipsing barefoot to the doctor's room. The nurse removed my borrowed nightie, looked through my hair and pushed my reluctant body towards the doctor, who seemed incredibly aged. He looked down my throat, my ears, surveyed my hands, turning them over and then thumped my chest. I let out a cry of resistance when he tried to inspect my bottom. The old doctor waved his hand as the nurse began to use force.

'Leave her, let her put her nightdress on.' I didn't mind the tears in front of him. 'Now don't look so worried, nobody's going to hurt you.'

'I'm not afraid of anything!' I yelled at him.

The old doctor clapped his hands. 'Good! Good! That's the

spirit! Sit down and blow your nose.' He handed me a large handkerchief, and took up a pad.

'Now, let's have your name.'

He poised his pen above the paper. I hesitated. I wanted to go home. What would they do to me? Would I go to prison? I didn't want to tell such a nice gentleman that I was a thief.

'Come, come. All right, have a good cry. Get it out, you'll feel much better.'

So I sobbed and heaved, and did feel much better.

'Let's start again and do tell me the truth, it's so much easier, eh?' he smiled encouragingly. 'What did you say your name was?'

'Marian Hughes,' I whispered. Well, now they knew. I felt a sense of relief.

'How old are you?'

'Eleven-and-a-quarter and I live at six-stroke-two, Westbourne Grove Terrace, W2. I live with my mother, sister and brother, older than me!' I'd gabbled it at breakneck speed.

He laughed. 'Hold on! Hold on!' Then he opened a drawer and passed me a boiled sweet. 'And school?'

'St Stevens,' I lied. Well, it was just down the road.

'Do you want to go home?'

'Oh, yes, please, when can I go?'

'It's not up to me.' My anxiety came flooding back. 'But I can make recommendations. Tell me, where did you get all those bruises and marks on your body?'

Lifting up my nightie, I inspected my legs. They did look pretty bashed.

'I'm always mucking about. Oh and we were bombed.'

'Tell me about the bombing.'

Bringing the date of the event forward, I gave a graphic account of the blast that had brought the ceiling down on Mummy's head. I missed out the cursing.

'Well, my dear, there's not much wrong with you. We need to

feed you up a bit. Go now and get dressed. You can join the other girls.'

'But I want to go home!'

'I expect you'll go in a few days.' He came round the desk and put his arm on my shoulders. 'And don't worry, everything will sort itself out, you'll see.' He called the nurse and I was allowed to dress and was taken to the playground.

Sliding easily back into the routine of institutional life over the next two weeks, I listened to the stories of the other girls, some of which were horrifying.

'I shouldn't be here,' volunteered a sad-eyed girl who disconcertingly took the seat opposite me at the table. 'They're going to hang me, I think. I hope they do it soon.'

I said nothing, not believing her.

But she persevered. 'My granddad hit me for as long as I remember. Hit my Mum too. I crashed him one with the backyard broom and he fell off his chair and bashed his head, and he's dead.'

'I'm sorry,' I said, sincerely.

She clasped her hands together above her elbows and leaned across the narrow table. 'I'm not. I'm glad. He'll not have a go at my Mum again.'

'They won't hang you. You're too young.' I touched her arm.

She suddenly took my hand and put it to her forehead and held on to it while she cried uncontrollably until a young matron gently eased her away from me.

Occasionally two of the girls would fight. The belligerents would be forcefully removed by two pairs of strong, practised hands and be locked away.

I looked forward to all mealtimes and to the glasses of milk in between. There were few books. I tried to read *What Katy Did* but I thought Katy a prat.

'Marian, your mother's here.'

Apprehension halted my steps.

'Come, don't you want to see her?'

'No! I mean yes!' I said helplessly. But there was no help for it, so I followed the matron into the office.

Mummy turned round and opened her arms. 'Oh my precious! I've been so worried! We searched everywhere!'

Entering into the spirit of the situation, I threw myself against her. She smelled lovely, but I felt the rigid boned corset under her new outfit. The fox fur draped over the shoulders of the ribbed sateen material of her neat, dark navy suit tickled her nose. The poor pointed little face of the fox was made into a clasp that attached to a hoop of silk on the base of its tail.

Then she took my hand in hers and held me at arms' length. High-heeled, red court shoes on her tiny feet matched the veiled, red pillbox hat set forward on her head. A tiny navy leather handbag hung on her arm and she was wearing neat leather gloves.

It seemed – unbelievably – that our home had been vetted and passed by social workers, who had been taken in by the tale of a poor child running in fear from the terrors of the raids and straight into trouble.

The taxi journey home, delightfully charged with laughter and mimicry of the hoodwinked authorities, brought Mummy and me close, both of us forgetting the misery that truly initiated the episode.

SIX

Camping

When we reached the top of the stairs, we had to climb over a great smelly heap. It turned out to be a tent, for we were to go camping. It transpired that Mummy had promised the social worker to remove us children to the country . . . to the safety of a friend's estate!

Dorothy's job had ended with the demolition of her office by a landmine. She sat enveloped in an indistinct fog, still awaiting her new glasses. Dorothy didn't really welcome me. I was hurt and a little sad that she was still angry with me for stealing. Perhaps she needed all her strength to protect herself. Anthony gave whoops of joy at my release.

Within an hour of the delivery of Dorothy's glasses, on a bright sunny day, we found ourselves on the Bayswater Road. We stood together expectantly with great bales of baggage. We were off to the Wye Valley. I gathered that it was hundreds of miles away in Wales, the land of my father. In my head was the singing of a thousand girls – 'Wales, Wales, sweet are thy hills and thy dales.'

Ecstatically happy, my arms lifted above my head, I joined Mummy in attracting attention from passing lorries. We were scattered along the pavement when a vehicle finally pulled up beside Mummy. The near-side door was flung open and

Mummy climbed up on to the step, and the next moment was beckoning urgently for us to bring up the baggage. She got down and the driver emerged after her, and I saw his look of dismay and hesitation on viewing us ragamuffins. Anthony and I charged towards him, dragging the load between us.

'Hang on,' the burly, pot-bellied man with the iron-grey hair shouted.' I can't take all this lot.'

Mummy held on to his arm. 'I'm taking these little orphans . . . Look at the poor mites.' Then she whispered something into his ear.

Before long we children were bouncing about in the back of the 'Harris's Sausages, Caln, Wilt's' lorry. Mummy sat in the cabin next to the driver. The three of us were locked in the back with the bundles.

'Smells of number twos,' said Anthony, attempting unsteadily to sniff the fresh air through the cracks in the back doors.

I pinched my nose and pulled an imaginary lavatory chain, making a farty noise as I did so.

'Shut up, you two. Let's make the best of it,' demanded Dorothy, who had created a regular throne out of the available boxes and sacks.

For a while I joined Anthony jumping and bucking in the near-empty area at the back but eventually we both settled next to Dorothy with our backs to the driver's cabin.

Out of London, we stopped at a lorry drivers' café, where the man treated us to enormous plates of food. Sausages, bacon, fried bread and mashed potatoes, spoiled only by a thick, brown, greasy gravy, which I found rather horrid. Followed by a deliciously stodgy bread pudding covered with a thin custard.

Over the table, the lorry driver looked at Mummy as if he were 'in love' with her, much to my amusement. After the meal, our stomachs bursting, he swung us all into the cabin of the lorry.

'Crikey. I'd take you all home with me if I had a decent place.'

He caressed my curls as he eyed the three of us with pity. 'To 'ell with it! I'll take you where you want to go.'

He reached over me and tried to put his arm round Dorothy, who stiffened. 'Get off me!' she cried, giving Mummy a look of disdain.

We arrived at Symonds Yat in the late afternoon. Our final destination was two miles further on, impassable for vehicles and only accessible on foot by the track alongside the river. We stretched ourselves with some relief. The lorry driver pressed all his money and most of his anatomy on us as he helped each of us down from the cab and placed us on the ground.

After climbing back into his vehicle, he sped away to cheers from Anthony and me; a 'God bless you' from Mummy; and a 'Rotten pig!' from Dorothy, for which she received a quick slap. I respected Dorothy's superior knowledge in all things, but was puzzled by her antagonism towards a generous spirit, being such herself.

Soon we were trundling along a sun-dappled path beside a rushing river with thick, dark forest on the other side of us. After travelling silently under the heavy loads for a while, we collapsed on to the river bank.

'Wow! We can go fishing,' said Anthony delightedly whooping as he spotted the large fish that seemed to leap over the whirlpools.

'Don't let anyone see you.' Mummy stood up and examined the rush of the river. 'The water looks very dangerous. In fact I don't want to catch you anywhere near the water,' she said, as she gently pulled Anthony away. I stood staring in awe of the great jagged cliffs on the opposite bank. 'Come on, dreamer. You can do that when you get there.'

Surely this is the place for 'Heaven on earth', I thought as we went through fields of lush grass, where cows stretched their necks and lowered their heads, eyeing us with intense curiosity as we passed. I was staggered at the beauty of their eyes, and astonished by the great ponderous-looking sack that hung between their legs that seemed to inhibit their progress as they staggered away from us. I'd seen cows in a picture book, I knew that milk came from cows, but this part of their anatomy had been omitted or had totally escaped my notice.

We carried on in silence. Mummy marched ahead with Anthony, carrying between them the enormous tent, which contained the bedding. I trailed far behind, dragging a large laundry basket, while Dorothy, utterly exhausted and protesting, wrenched her bundle angrily across the coarse ground behind me.

'This is madness,' she exclaimed.

'Cheer up, Dorothy,' I called.

'Bloody cheer up yourself,' she snapped back.

I was truly shocked. Dorothy was almost perfection. She never swore; she never complained. I dragged the basket a little further, then sat on it and waited for her. I thought how frail she looked. She started yelling at me.

'You're a thief,' she screamed. 'You'll go to hell.'

'Don't you like me any more, Dorothy?' I couldn't bear the pain of her evident disapproval.

'Do you expect me to? You get arrested as a common thief. I was sick with worry. All the *lies* we told, just because of you!'

I examined a cowpat, already drying at the edges. 'I didn't mean to be caught.'

'Stupid! If you steal, you'll get caught. You'll always get caught. You're heading towards becoming a thoroughly bad lot. You've got no conscience about it either, that's what beats me.'

'But half the time we've nothing to eat.' I looked at my hands. 'Besides, you eat the stuff. I've seen you eat it.' I stole a look at Dorothy.

'Well, don't think it doesn't choke me! The thought of what's going to happen to Anthony . . . he wouldn't steal by himself . . . it's *you* who puts him up to it . . . you always were a trouble . . . I can't stand the craziness . . . you don't know how decent people live . . . I'm ashamed of you all . . . you know our mother's mad, don't you? . . . she'll get *worse*, you know . . . I can't stand her. Look at yourself! Look at those rags you're wearing. . . .'

Surveying what I could see of myself, I thought I looked all right. I often poked through Mummy's things for something, and with the aid of a safety pin managed to sport a new outfit which would be worn for a week or two.

'Oh Dorothy! I think I look nice.'

Dorothy's rage subsided. Suddenly, she was contrite.

'Oh you do, you do. I'm just a meanie. You're the prettiest urchin this side of the river.'

We heard a yell from Anthony ahead of us. He waved and I saw there was a man with him.

'There,' said Dorothy, 'I just prayed that you wouldn't have to take that basket one step further.'

She took both my hands and confronted me with great earnestness. 'You must pray to Jesus! He really does answer prayers. You mustn't steal any more! Will you promise me, now?'

Pleased that the anger between us had passed, I replied sincerely. 'I will pray, and I'll never take anything again.'

We lifted Dorothy's bundle between us, and walked happily ahead of the man who puffed and muttered as he staggered behind with the basket on his back.

The farm stank. A great wet heap was steaming right outside the entrance, almost touching the walls of the farmhouse, which were stained by previous, larger heaps.

'Why do you keep it so close to the house?' I asked the farmer's wife who stood laughing at our cries of 'Pooh!'

'It'll keep off the east wind and warm the sitting-room in winter. We always have a pile of it.'

Dorothy cried, 'But how can you bear the smell of it?'

The farmer's wife smiled. 'You'll not be smelling it yourselves very soon.'

And sure enough after we'd been given a very frugal meal of two thin pieces of Spam, dry bread and a mug of milk each, we were no longer aware of it.

Soon we were struggling to erect the tent on the edge of a field. It was half rotten and full of holes, and Mummy was cursing the chap who'd given it to her for nothing. It was almost dark when, exhausted, we finally settled down.

The screeching of an owl woke me. It was pitch dark except for the glow of Mummy's cigarette. She was sitting like an Indian, cross-legged and very still.

'Mummy, what are you thinking of?' I whispered.

'Hush now, don't wake the others.'

'Tell me what you're always thinking?' I insisted.

'I was thinking of George. He's your new father!'

'I don't want a father.'

Exasperated, Mummy snapped, 'Be quiet and go to sleep.'

Lying quite still, I watched the glow of the cigarette. The thought of this 'George' joining us made me feel miserable, without knowing quite why. I'd not been used to men at close quarters. The old A.R.P. chaps were special. They were as mischievous as Anthony and me. They didn't seem like 'men' at all. I prayed to Jesus, not really expecting Him to answer my prayers, for I was very conscious of my wickedness. I prayed that George would never come back from the war, that I wouldn't steal again and that we'd all be happy, and finally I drifted back to sleep.

We awoke to find everything sodden. Although the night had been warm, heavy dew had crept through the rotten ground-sheet and the holes in the roof of the tent.

Outside, Anthony and I called to each other to see this or that wonder of nature. We both agreed that this was the perfect life.

'Go and get some paraffin from the farm,' Mummy shouted.

We raced each other until we reached the farmhouse where the cows were laboriously waddling towards the milking parlour.

The farmer shook his fist at us.

'Now, don't you two start being pests, or he'll get a stick to you!' the farmer's wife said, as she came into view.

'We weren't doing anything!' Anthony pleaded. 'Can we help with the cows? We've come for paraffin. Mummy sent us.'

'She did, did she? And what are you going to put it in?' she exclaimed.

Nevertheless, she eventually gave us a rusty tin, all the while protesting that money wouldn't come amiss.

Back at the tent, Anthony was sent again to the farm for eggs and milk, with money this time. The wonderful primus stove, prepared with sweet-smelling methylated spirit, was pumped vigorously till it burst into a minor roar.

By the time the water boiled Anthony returned.

'The old man wouldn't give us any eggs and they were eating *millions* for breakfast!' he said ruefully. 'He asked about our ration books.'

'Damn the ration books,' said Mummy crossly. 'Perhaps you could do some work up there. Work for eggs and maybe some vegetables as well. Go and ask the farmer's wife, I think she's a Londoner. He grunts like an animal.' We all laughed. 'He must be twenty years older than her.'

After breakfast, which ended up being the stale bread and pickings we'd gathered together from home, Dorothy and Anthony set off to the village stores, while I stayed behind to help mend the tent. I was proud of my handiwork and pleased at Mummy's surprise discovery of my talents, which included rigging up lines to hang out the bedding.

'You're not just a dreamer after all.' She smiled warmly. 'In fact I think you're quite a clever little thing.'

61

I basked in the rays of approval. The sun was warm and Mummy was happy. I was spurred onwards by treats of rare praise. We talked, laughed and sang songs together as we sewed on coloured patches. I felt I could live forever in a tent in this lovely valley, which was so peaceful, the air so fresh, and Mummy so prettily sitting cross-legged squinting at her needle.

There was magic about Mummy. At this moment I experienced exquisite joy. I thought how sad it was that such times were often bridged by uncontrollable rage, a torment not understood by me, but vaguely accepted as one might the fierce, frightening energy of attack from a wounded animal.

'You're looking so serious, and right through me. You're giving me the shivers!' Mummy laughed. 'What can you see?'

Hesitating for only a moment, I said, 'I see the prettiest lady in all the world and the cleverest!'

We both laughed, then Mummy held out a crooked little finger which I entwined with mine and pulled. The resulting fart sent both of us rolling about hysterically giggling.

'Mummy, tell me about Daddy.'

Her face clouded as she hugged her knees, with a theatrical far-away expression.

'He was the sweetest, gentlest man in the world. He worshipped me. Your Daddy Jim worshipped the ground I trod on!'

I wanted to ask: Why then did he kill himself? Instead I just said, 'Why did he die?'

Mummy jumped up and pushed the question away, 'T.B., my love. He just got sick and died, leaving me to bring you four up. For God's sake, those two have been gone for hours.'

The spell of intimacy was broken and, as if in sympathy, the sun went behind the black clouds that raced across the sky. We looked up together and together pulled the bundles into the shelter. Dorothy and Anthony ducked into the tent just as a terrific downpour, accompanied by rolling thunder, swamped us.

The rest of that day was spent drying everything out and cooking a marvellous meal.

Occasionally we would go to a nearby town to collect money that rarely arrived. The money was apparently from George. It was never much and most of it would go on cigarettes and the rent for our London flat. Frequently we didn't have enough to eat.

Anthony and I wandered around the countryside foraging, and never came back empty handed. Although normally a dairy and forestry area, scraps of land everywhere were under food crops and many vegetables were ripening in the late August sun. 'Dig for Victory' was the motto. The eye of a chicken sitting upon an egg is a fearsome thing when viewed by a common thief. But a 'please' and a 'thank you' softened my guilt.

These activities were encouraged by Mummy who often sent me to beg for a little money or cigarettes. I enjoyed these escapades as one would a 'dare'. Dorothy protested that my character would be further damaged, and Anthony agreed with her, thereby relieving himself of begging duties. It seemed to me that Dorothy almost thought that begging was worse than stealing. Considering that Jesus said, 'Ask and it shall be given unto you . . .', well, I didn't feel any shame.

My bright approach to a young man in a light blue uniform was received with a startled look of dismay. He was pale and thin, with the uncomprehending look of a lost soul. He hurried away from me and seemed to lurch forward with unseeing eyes over a protruding turf, going down with a thump. As I ran to help him up, he frightened me by giving a groan, and raising his arm as if to protect himself from me.

'They give me the creeps!' Mummy shivered as a group of pale-blue uniformed young men passed. 'You shouldn't talk to them. They should hide them away.'

'But why are they like that?' I asked.

'Shell shocked! Poor . . . now don't look so miserable about things that don't concern you!'

I started to think about the war. I hadn't taken much notice of anything except the air raids. The austerity and shortages that people were going on about meant nothing to me after the prim life at the Orphanage. So many wonderful things were available. I'd seen newsreels, but somehow I hadn't been interested; the here-and-now discovery of my immediate environment was enough.

The tent rotted visibly and began to rip at the seams. The hot sun, wind and rain in constant rotation made repair ineffective. Now it had rained for days and Mummy sat in the dampness, shut off from us and hardly moving. We'd been here for a month and Dorothy wanted to go home. Then at last, the sun shone and the three of us set off further than ever in our exploration of the countryside.

We crossed the land as the crow flies, avoiding roads which were full of military vehicles. Eventually we found ourselves in a restricted area.

'Wow! Just look at those tents!' Anthony cried out.

'Shush! Be quiet,' I whispered.

As if a plan had been formulated between us in an instant, we fell into the long grass. It was still early in the morning and we lay for some time watching the soldiers moving about.

'They'll think we're spies!' Anthony giggled.

Stealing a look at Dorothy, expecting any moment that she'd call a halt to our fancy, I saw only a look of determination. No word of intention passed between us, but we had all three made up our minds. We were going to have one of those beautiful tents.

We slid silently sideways around the encampment until we were aware of a man singing. 'I don't want to set the world on fire . . . I just want to start . . . a flame in your heart. . . .' He was standing at a little mirror, shaving, his braces hanging over his trousers, his legs crossed in an effort to keep them up. He seemed to gyrate slowly to the rhythm of his song as the mirror gently swayed from a branch of a tree. I'd never seen a man shave before, and stifled giggles at this ludicrous, yet fascinating, scene.

We watched him as he ducked in and out of his tent, until he finally emerged smartly dressed. He stood taking deep breaths, then raised his left elbow and placed two fingers under his nose, whipped his right hand rigidly above his head and barked: 'Heil Hitler!' and marched off. The three of us exploded into uncontrollable laughter. Fortunately, he didn't hear us as he was 'Trrum . . bom . . trrum . . bom . . bom'ing at the top of his voice. The tent he had left was secluded and set apart from the rest.

We crept on all fours towards it. It was beautiful! It was enormous! It was round! Inside, it seemed even more spacious. Neat and tidy, there was little in it apart from the bed, a table, a chair and a rickety chest of drawers.

Dorothy sat on the bed. 'We can't shift this!' she said hopelessly. 'We couldn't even lift it, and we must be miles away!'

Puzzling for a while, I said slowly, 'We could roll it up and drag it by the guy ropes.'

Anthony cried. 'That's it! We could just roll it! It must weigh a ton, but the three of us could roll it. We could, Dorothy! I know we could.'

'Oh I couldn't! We shouldn't! It would be so wicked!' Dorothy lamented. 'That poor man. He'd have such a shock.'

I giggled and Anthony said: 'He sure would! Oh come on, Dorothy, they've got lots and lots of tents.'

'I'm surprised at you, Anthony!' Her face clouded, she took off her glasses and rubbed her face violently. 'We could get caught.' She sat silently for a moment, then jumped up smiling broadly. 'Let's do it!'

The three of us ran round the tent and, pulling with all our might, released the pegs. As we did so, we saw a wheelbarrow nearby.

'It's a gift from God!' exclaimed Dorothy.

Panting and groaning as we struggled, in no time at all we had the thing collapsed. Suddenly we heard voices! All three of us ducked under the tent, now strewn upon the ground. I felt my heart thumping and pumping in my head as we lay not daring to move. We heard the footsteps of two men. Then they stopped.

The men stood laughing. 'Would you believe it? The silly bugger!' said one. 'Shall we tell him?' said the other. 'No, let him find out in the dark!' and off they went.

We crept out in a state of shock.

Dorothy went to make a run for it. 'Come on, they may be back in a minute!'

'No! No, Dorothy! We've almost got it!' I wasn't going to give up so easily. We fell upon the tent again, Anthony trying to screw it up impossibly. 'No, Anthony! We'll have to do it neatly or we won't be able to.'

We were getting jumpy, and I forgot to be quiet. Dorothy spoke through her teeth, 'For Heaven's sake keep your voice down!'

Eventually we managed to roll the thing up into a ball and, first throwing in the pegs, got it into the wheelbarrow. Then we covered it with leaves and twigs so that it seemed we had a great mound of firewood. Off we trundled in a rather crazy fashion, exhausted and fearful.

It was downhill all the way, and we had to pull with all our might, for it seemed that the wheelbarrow would run away from us. We left the camp area and now came to the ditch we had previously just jumped over by way of an earth-covered pipe. We waved incessantly at the soldiers who, calling and whistling at us, seemed to be everywhere.

The brute overturned many times, and we began to think that

we'd never reach our destination. Although very tired and not having eaten all day, still we zig-zagged on. Eventually we had to confess that we were lost and, leaving the path, lay down and fell asleep.

I awoke to the sounds of splitting wood and saw a young man of incredible stature wielding an axe. Dorothy shoved me. 'Ask him the way.'

I got up, smoothing the leaves off me, and went over to him. 'Excuse me, Sir,' I said most politely. 'Could you please tell us the way to Symonds Yat?'

He looked at me blankly, then he laughed, throwing back his head. He took hold of a sapling and thwacked it with the axe, severing it with one blow. He then held it aloft with a joyously triumphant air and threw it like a lance towards a pile of branches.

'Big Joe!' He pointed to himself.

Dorothy was now standing at my side. 'How do you do, Big Joe?' she enquired.

'Nicely, nicely!'

Again she asked him the way, he merely puffed out his chest and flexed his arms. 'Big Joe strong!'

Anthony dragged the wheelbarrow over to him. 'Could you please take our tent to the Biblings farm for us? We can't take it any further.'

Big Joe gathered up the great tent and hoisted it on to the nape of his neck with ease and immediately set off. Anthony collected up the pegs in his skimpy jacket, leaving the wheel-barrow where it stood, and the three of us ran after the young giant who seemed to take seven-league steps.

Dorothy looked up at the sky. 'Thank you, dear Jesus!'

We *stole* the tent! I thought, smugly happy that Dorothy had sunk to my level, and even had the cheek to thank Jesus for her sins.

Dorothy trailed far behind. 'Wait, Big Joe, oh wait!'

Big Joe turned and I pointed to the figure of Dorothy. Without putting down the tent, he went back and scooped her up, and she clung to him the rest of the way until we reached the farm. Here he gently placed her on the ground and put the tent next to her.

'Oh down there in the field, please take it down there!' Dorothy pointed frantically.

But the farmer's wife had come out, hearing the commotion.

'Joe Lark, what are you doing here?' she shouted crossly to him. Big Joe turned and fled. 'Great idiot lout!' she grumbled. 'Don't you have anything to do with him. He's a time waster.'

She pointed to the khaki heap. 'What's that you've got there?'

'It's our new tent!' I answered quickly. 'We wanted Big Joe to take it down to the field for us!'

'Then you should have asked him to,' she snapped.

Dorothy was exasperated. 'We did, but you made him go away!'

'I made him? I made him?' she said in mock surprise and shuffled into her kitchen muttering, banging the door behind her.

The three of us stared at the thing ruefully, then got together, pushing and rolling it across the track and into the field. The field ran fairly steeply towards the river and the great bundle gathered momentum. We ran with it whooping and yelling towards Mummy who, hearing our cries, was standing with her arm shielding her eyes from the evening sun. To our relief, she was dressed. When we reached the tent, it was tidy and, to our delight, we smelled stew bubbling over the primus.

Over the meal, amid shrieks of laughter, we related all that had happened in the day. She hugged us and wanted to erect the tent there and then, but all three of us were ready only for sleep.

The following morning, the tent was up, mightily supreme. The old tent served as a groundsheet.

*

We were more comfortable now, although the chill of nightfall tucked us into bed earlier. Anthony helped the surly old farmer every morning, in return for eggs, once even a chicken, and all the milk we could drink. We became strong. Anthony seemed to shoot up and Dorothy's cheeks were prettily rosy.

I had worms. I discovered them when squatting in a field. Tiny little white worms, that squiggled tortuously and died immediately after exposure to air. They looked glistening and clean in themselves, I pondered, as I examined them with great interest. If anything, I felt a little sorry for them. I once counted thirty-four with the aid of a twig. I reasoned that I must have had them for a considerable time, for my bottom had itched for ages. More than once Mummy had cuffed me for the disgusting habit of scratching, so I learned to do this secretly. Sometimes a powerful urge would have me hopping about from one foot to another. 'Keep still, for God's sake!' Mummy would cry. I was not prepared to tell my secret for fear of a clinical inspection, but I guessed that pangs of hunger had something to do with the presence of worms.

Another month passed happily. The water bailiff chased Anthony, who could now catch fish with comparative ease. He and I stole rabbits from the farmer's snares. The farmer's wife gave us, though grudgingly, some clothes left by last year's campers. She'd kept them for they'd paid her to send them on, but she lost their address. 'They'll be grown out of them and there's no sense in waste!'

Dorothy was now restless and miserable. She wanted to go back to London to pursue her career. The late October frosts numbed her into staying in bed most of the morning.

When eventually we left the lovely valley, we charged the farmer's wife with the care of the army tent and assured her that we would claim it the following year.

SEVEN

Loss

After taking the bus from Symonds Yat, we stood waiting outside the post office at Ross-on-Wye, where Mummy was to collect some money. The three of us heard raised voices coming from inside, and sure enough Mummy emerged in a rage. There was no money, she had none, and not one of us fancied the trials of hitching on empty stomachs. I already wished that we hadn't left the valley. We sat on a bench while Mummy went off to try to rustle up some money.

'I'm leaving as soon as we get to London,' Dorothy announced. 'I'll take a job in service if I have to!' She looked around. 'Do we look normal? I hate her, I do!'

I resented that. 'You shouldn't hate anyone, except the Germans.' Then I remembered. 'Love your enemies. . . .'

'Would you love the Germans if they came here?' said Anthony.

Dorothy slid up to the other end of the bench, retiring into sullen silence, hugging herself and disowning us two ragamuffins. Anthony and I discussed what we'd do if the Germans invaded.

'We'd be saboteurs! We'd set fire to everything! Well, I'd do that and you can run messages,' he said in a superior manner.

'I can light a fire better than you can anytime!' I said resentfully. 'Besides, they'd never suspect a sweet little girl.' I stretched myself into a pose and flickered my eyelids.

'Shut up, you two, you make me sick,' said Dorothy crossly.

We fell into unaccustomed bickering, until Mummy turned up. She was on the arm of an army sergeant.

'Come on, you lot! We're going to eat!'

Dorothy refused to leave the seat. She burst into tears. 'Oh my! You've just picked him up!' The hatred showed in her face.

'Oh come, darling. Ronnie's an old friend!' She turned to him. 'How long is it? Must be years!'

'They all yours?' Ronnie looked uncomfortable.

'Do you think I'd have that one around if she wasn't?' said Mummy spitefully. 'Come on, Miss Prissy Prim!' She put a finger under Dorothy's chin. Dorothy shook herself away.

'Look,' said the embarrassed Ronnie. 'I think I'd better go, I'm sorry, but your daughter don't take to me. Here, get the kids some grub.' He handed Mummy some money and marched off in a hurry, much to our relief.

'Did you really know him, Mummy?' I enquired.

'Of course I did, you silly. As for you Dorothy, you make me ashamed! What a way to treat an old friend of mine. You've a long way to go, you dirty-minded little prig!'

People were staring at us. For a moment, it looked as if Mummy was about to hit Dorothy. I took her hand. 'Come on, Mummy, let's eat!'

The grinding in my stomach just begged for food!

Dorothy's anger dissipated over the meal of scrambled dried eggs on toast, after which we made our way to the railway station. On the train we noticed that the names of the stations had been blotted out. Anthony said that it was to confuse spies, who might land by parachute. As we neared London, the train slowed, and we saw the enormous devastation which had been inflicted by the raids on our great city. We watched it grimly. For the first time I briefly felt a hint of apprehension, then the other passengers started singing: 'There'll always be an England. And England shall be free. . . .' We ended the journey with our spirits unconquerable.

Anthony and I raced each other up the stairs, pleased to be home again.

Before the week was out, Dorothy had left us. She did indeed go into service.

Mummy lost her that job by interfering and begging Dorothy's employer for money, much to Dorothy's shame. Dorothy told us that Mummy had tried to drag her away, all the time shouting abuse. She said she'd screamed to be left alone to get on with her own life.

She got another position, looking after little children. Now we hardly ever saw her. Sometimes Anthony and I found her waiting in the street for us, always with something to eat. We missed her terribly. We hadn't appreciated all the kind things she had done for us.

The flat was in filthy disarray and Mummy had taken to her bed again. Dorothy was on a purposeful visit. I skipped off with the Marmite sandwich she had brought me, but Anthony huddled in conversation with her. He was fed up and talked about going back to school.

'I want to be an engineer,' he confided to me later.

'Anthony, you don't mean it!' I hesitated. 'I want you to be an engineer, but *school*?' Even the word filled me with disgust.

'Dorothy says there's that job on the board outside the baker's. I'm going after that too.' He sounded defiant.

'Oh, Anthony,' I said sadly.

'Cheer up! Baker's, get it?' A grin lit his face. 'Grub! Cakes! I've got method in my madness, you silly.'

'Oh let's go now!'

'Why not?'

We crept out of the flat and down the first two flights of stairs, and then pelted down the rest to the street door, where Anthony fished his half-comb from his pocket and attempted to run it through his unruly brown hair. Then he playfully licked his fingers, smoothed his eyebrows, finishing his toilet by lifting one foot and then the other, spitting on his shoes, and rubbing them on the back of his socks.

He spread his arms in a grand pose. 'Do I look a million dollars, or don't I?'

'You look beautiful,' I said with true admiration as we set off down the road.

I waited for ages outside the baker's shop after Anthony disappeared inside. There was nothing much displayed in the window. A cardboard wedding cake caught my fancy, but just then a barrel-shaped, unshaved, droopy-eyed man, on tiny legs, came out of the shop and removed the 'Wanted' sign from the board. He gave me a suspicious stare, so I eased myself to the other end of the shop window.

I became conscious of a rush of warm air and found myself looking down through a wide iron grill set into the pavement into a littered basement yard. I knelt and tried to peer into the open window below.

Anthony popped his head out of the window and whispered: 'Got the job. It's smashing! See you,' and ducked inside.

Three hours later he arrived home, red-eyed, exhausted and covered from head to foot with a fine dusting of flour.

He held out a blue sugar bag to Mummy. She peered inside and took out three small misshapen cakes.

'For Christ's sake! Is that all?' she exploded.

'I get seven shillings and sixpence a week, and food.' He pointed to the cakes. 'That's the food.' Then he drew cakes from his sleeves. 'And these.' And from under his jumper. 'And these.'

We ended up laughing uncontrollably, with a great pile of cakes to consume between us.

A few days later Anthony sneaked me into the baker's shop after closing time. The basement was an absolute mess. Grey flour was caked on the walls and the ceiling, from which hung a single, naked, dusty bulb. Enormous sacks, a size I'd never seen before, were treacherously stacked at one end. Boxes, some empty, some with packets of lard, and others containing a various assortment of tins, were balanced precariously against the other wall. But the most evil thing I saw was the enormous sieve loosely suspended from the ceiling by flat wooden slats. Upon the sieve were thousands of little wiggling worms.

'Yuck!' I pulled a face. 'Don't tell me these come out of the flour?'

Anthony grinned. 'They're weevils.' He picked up a handful and held them under the light. 'Look, those little dark ones? They're babies. These lovely fat white ones must be mummies and daddies. Ain't they sweet?'

'People eat this?'

'There's a war on. I'm learning all about flour. I bet I'll be an expert soon. You know, we grow this stuff. Before the war they just fed it to animals.'

'Where did we get our flour before the war?'

'From America, or Canada. Or Timbuktu,' he laughed.

Then we sang together:

> Germany was Hungary
> Ate a bit of Turkey
> On a bit of China
> Dipped in Greece.
> Long legged Italy
> Kicked poor Sicily
> Right into the middle
> Of the Mediterranean Sea . . .'

A voice barked down the grill.

'You working, boy?'

We heard the man opening the shop door. I hid behind the sacks in the dimmest corner. Steps hippety-hopped down the stairs. He burst into the basement, charged up to Anthony, and slapped him hard round the head.

'You done nothin'! I give you plenty something, you don't hurry up.' He moved round the room slowly inspecting everything. I made myself invisible. Then I heard a grating sound. I peered out of my hiding place and saw he'd opened a large door I hadn't noticed through which came an instant gush of heat. He threatened Anthony again and left.

'He just came to check the ovens, the rotten old pig!' said Anthony, rubbing his head. Then brightly, 'Here's what I do.'

He lifted a measure of flour with a large silver scoop which he held with both hands, and placed it in the sieve which was the size of a large dustbin lid. With both arms held out in front of him, he pushed it backwards and forwards vigorously. When the sieve was heavy with weevils, he climbed up two sacks and released two of the slats from their hook in the ceiling, enabling him to tip the contents of the sieve into an empty flour-sack.

I stood in admiration.

'Here,' he said. 'Ever tasted this stuff?'

He was prising the lid off a wooden barrel that he'd dragged under the light.

'It looks like tar,' I said doubtfully.

'It's molasses. It's what sugar comes from,' he said authoritatively.

We wiped a flat stick upon my dress, and then dipped it into the barrel. Anthony encouraged me to taste the stuff. I gave a tentative lick. Soon we were both laughing and avidly lapping both sides of the stick.

'Now you'd better scarper. I must get on with this. My arms

ache when I stop but I'll be as strong as a horse by the time I've finished. Hang on, I'll nick some cakes.'

He disappeared into the other room and, returning, filled my proffered skirt, which I then clasped to me. I followed him up the stairs and he let me out on to the street.

Anthony's cakes about his person were soon discovered. The man beat him. Nothing daunted, Anthony took to standing on boxes and passing his offerings to me through the filthy street gratings.

One evening, he forgot to replace the lid on the molasses barrel and drowned mice were discovered. The man merely removed them by their tails and threw them in with the weevils. He replaced the lid. He then clouted Anthony and dismissed him.

Soon Anthony and I were up to our old tricks. We'd wander the streets in aimless pursuits, stealing what took our fancy.

One day we went into a sweet shop and I asked angelically if the assistant would tell me the time. As the poor fellow went into the back room, we grabbed at what was immediately in front of us. For Anthony, a carton of tiny packets of chewing gum, while my hands closed about a charity box. I instantly wished that I could put it back.

Urgent shouts forced us to split. Anthony hugging the carton, spewing the little packets as he ran, fled one way. I cast away the charity box, which beat like a drum in tune to my racing feet as I went in the opposite direction. I got clean away and went to wait for Anthony at our hidy-hole in a bombed building, where we often consumed our spoils.

I waited and waited. He didn't appear.

Fearfully, I kept picturing the trail he had left. I knew he'd been caught! Oh the misery I felt! Poor Anthony, sweet gentle boy! 'Oh come *on* Anthony!' I wailed aloud, but Anthony didn't come.

Finally I made my way home.

'That you two?' Mummy called. 'Go and get some cigarettes, please.'

'It's just me,' I said quietly.

I reached for the money.

Mummy grabbed my hand and swung me down on to the bed.

'Where's Anthony?'

'I don't know!' I said, turning my head away from her.

She noticed my tear-stained face and a look of alarm crept over her. 'What do you mean, you don't know?'

'Oh, we just quarrelled a bit, and he went off.'

'Oh, is that all?' She slumped back on her bed, dismissing me with a wave of her hand. 'Just hurry with the cigarettes, won't you?'

I looked up and down Westbourne Grove, straining to catch sight of Anthony. 'Please! Please Jesus, send him back!' I prayed, wiping my smarting eyes with the back of my hand.

After buying the cigarettes, I dawdled about for at least an hour until my brain began to work again. 'Perhaps they'll send him to a remand home, like the one they'd sent me to,' I thought. It then occurred to me in a rush that they wouldn't let him home unless the social worker passed the flat.

Grasping at the thought, I raced home. I knew I had to clean up. As I turned into the front door, I almost crashed into Mummy, whose white face startled me. A policeman followed her. She gave me a terrible look as she snatched the cigarettes and pushed me aside without a word. Then she followed the policeman into a waiting car, which did a wild three-point turn and sped away.

Not knowing that the policeman had already seen the state of the flat, I set about tidying and scrubbing, and created a mighty dust-up as I swept the carpet. Then I tackled the kitchen, washing up and cleaning the gas stove with the aid of handfuls of soda until my fingers resembled little sponges. By now it was dark, but I'd remembered to put up the black-out curtains in the windows. Seeing that it was only eight-thirty, I decided to have a go at the enormous amount of washing I'd thrown into the bath.

I put the kettle on and then grated a bar of Sunlight soap into a small bowl, to which I added the hot water, before mixing it into the washing in the bath. Then removing my socks and shoes and hoisting my dress, I climbed into the bath and started marching up and down, singing at the top of my voice. My brilliant idea worked! The water became grey and gritty at the bottom. I changed the water and, tired out, left the lot to soak overnight. I made myself a cup of cocoa in the kitchen.

Idle once more, I thought of Anthony, and resisted an almost overwhelming impulse to return to a state of misery.

I was never to see Anthony again.

Pushing aside such thoughts, I carefully washed my cup and tidied Mummy's room. It was now ten-thirty, well past bedtime and still she hadn't returned. It occurred to me in an instant that she would come home in a fury. Quickly, I went to my room, slipping off my clothes in a sudden panic. I jumped into bed and watched the clouds flitting across the moon through the criss-crossed window, and fell asleep.

I awoke suddenly, to see Mummy standing over me, wild-eyed in the moonlight. Poised above my head was a large kitchen knife held in her two fists with the point downwards. Strangely, I felt no fear. I just closed my eyes and waited. A calmness and peacefulness possessed me. Not one whit of terror passed through me when, at last, I heard a low groan and a swish as Mummy left the room. Nor was there any feeling of relief. I lay for a while thinking it had been a dream.

But in the morning the big knife clattered off the bed on to the floor. Fearful that the noise would disturb Mummy, I silently retrieved it and replaced it in the kitchen.

With a cup of tea, I gently tiptoed to her room, opening the door ever so quietly, but found her still asleep. Looking out through the frosty window of the sitting-room, I sipped the tea, feeling lonely and sorry for yesterday's events. Everything was so quiet. There was no Anthony to break the silence with grimacing whispers or stifled jubilation, when picking over the scraps in the kitchen.

I heard Mummy coughing, and dashed into the kitchen with the empty cup. Was she still asleep? With trepidation, for I could not bear the stillness, I called to her. 'Tea, Mummy? I've brought you tea!'

I crept into her room. She slowly turned over, motioned me to place the cup next to her, and unexpectedly swept me into her arms where I sobbed my heart out.

'Hey, come, now! It's all my fault,' she said bitterly.

'I'm sorry, Mummy!'

'God help me! I tried!' Tearfully she raised a clenched fist above her. 'I tried!' she yelled. 'I'm bleeding to death!'

'Are you hurt?'

I felt anxious, but her tears turned to a smile.

'Ah, my little love.' She sighed. 'It's every woman's fate!'

'Have your tea.'

Eventually she told me about Anthony. It seemed that he would appear in court and a Care and Protection order would be made, with a recommendation that Mummy was an 'unfit person'.

Anthony had stated that he didn't want to go home.

A few days later, Mummy came home from the court looking grey and weary. She tossed off her clothes, leaving them strewn around, and donned her now grubby but newish Chinese dressing-gown, and got into bed.

'What happened? What happened to Anthony?'

'They won't let me see him. They've sent him to some God-forsaken Approved School. They won't tell me where, but I'll find him. By God I'll find him! They can't take my children away again!'

'You've still got me, Mummy!' I wept. 'I'll never leave you!'

But I was dismissed with, 'Make me some tea.'

When I brought it to her, I saw with terror her spill out several aspirins and swallow them. I remembered Dorothy saying that the whole bottle would kill you. I removed it while smoothing the covers, then stole out of the room.

In the kitchen, I fished around for something to eat. There was nothing except a little egg powder, which I mixed with milk and sugar. I was so hungry! I wanted bread! I decided to go out and pick up something.

Cautiously, I went some distance from home, and I was soon stopping people in the street.

'Excuse me. Could you please tell me if I'm on the right road for Twickenham?' I asked politely.

Inevitably, the passer-by stated that Twickenham was a long way away, and why did I want to go there?

'Mummy was taken to hospital,' I lied, hoping that I looked sufficiently sad, 'and I have to go to my aunty's, I . . . I lost my bus fare!'

I'd begged dozens of times before and I thought people measly if I only got three pence or so. Responsible citizens boringly suggested the police station. Occasionally, some good soul unhesitatingly gave me a shilling. I used to dress in one of Mummy's 1930s crêpe dresses, tucked up around the waist, so hanging at various lengths around the hem, with a vast cardigan and Anthony's grey boys' socks. Despite my blonde hair and blue eyes, I would sometimes be mistaken for a gypsy.

But it just wasn't the same without Anthony. I became nervous of approaching people and had to summon up all my courage. There was no one to laugh with or share the spoils. I suddenly found myself uncertain, even shy, and my voice came in a whisper. I'd leave it today. Two and fourpence. Cigarettes for Mummy and the rest on food. When it came to it, I stole the cigarettes while buying only a stick of barley sugar. I fancied butter, but you had to have a ration book for that. For some reason, we didn't seem to have ration books; I thought Mummy had sold them. I managed to buy a small tin of golden syrup and went into the grocers' to see if I could steal anything. There was a queue. Two women had their beady eyes upon me with an air of suspicious distaste. I contented myself by making one of them uncomfortable with a long stare.

In Pritchard's, the bread shop, there was talk of bread rationing, and the queue was extra long. Attention was focused on an argument between three women over the ethics of the black market. Their hostility was directed towards a 'posh' lady, dripping with jewellery, with a funny hat, a fox fur draped around her shoulders. She had been refused more than one loaf of bread, and she'd said huffily that she knew where she could get anything she wanted. While all eyes were centred upon her, I took the opportunity to stuff several rolls down the front of my dress, and made my way home.

'That you, Marian?' Mummy called.

Delighted that she was awake, I charged into the bedroom.

'What do you think you look like?' Mummy laughed to see my bulging bosoms.

I tipped the contents on to her bed, rolls, syrup and the cigarettes which she pounced upon.

'God knows! You'll be following Anthony at this rate!' Her smile faded. She looked pasty and tired.

'Shall I make you some more tea? Will you have a roll?' I was already tearing at one.

'No, darling. Well perhaps I'll have the tea.' She delved about the bed, pulling back the covers. 'Have you seen my aspirins?'

I saw a great stain of blood. Panic seized me. 'Mummy! Mummy! What's happened?'

'I'm ill, darling. I hope to God I'll be dead soon.'

In horror I cried out: 'No Mummy! No! Don't leave me!'

My long hair was smoothed off my face. 'Don't worry, darling. I'll be all right in a few days.' She smiled, playfully pushing my head. 'I didn't mean to frighten you. I shan't die. You love me, don't you?'

'Yes, Mummy, I do.'

She sounded really surprised. 'Yes, I really think you do! I thank God for it! Anthony didn't want to see me and Dorothy had nothing but hate for me. She has a cold little heart. She really hurt me!' She lay looking up at the ceiling. 'She was the sweetest baby. I idolised her. She was so bright . . . so affectionate . . . she leaves me with a stone in my heart.'

I stopped her. 'Mummy. Mummy, it's just that she was scared of you. She missed the Orphanage. We never had any money. She was just upset all the time. I'm sure she loves you really.' I tried to placate her.

Mummy writhed in an obvious spasm of pain. 'Find the aspirins,' she demanded.

I brought them, made the tea, and left her to sleep. After wandering silently around the flat, I discovered *Three Men in a Boat*, glad that I had somehow overlooked the book before. Some hours later I heard Mummy, swishing water about in the bathroom, and saw her bending naked over the bath washing out her bedding.

'Mummy, leave it. I'll do that.'

She snatched a towel and wound it around herself. 'No, don't touch it!' Then she sped into her room, emerging in a short time, fully dressed.

She held up a half-crown. 'Come on, my girl. Let's go and eat!' We had a feast of fish and chips. Oddly, I hadn't known it was such a tasty dish. I hated the smell of butcher's shops, pubs and fish-and-chip shops. I held my breath as I passed.

Mummy's mood brightened, and on the way home we passed the Roxy cinema. I dashed over to look at the stills.

'Fancy it?' she smiled. I almost jumped for joy.

An air raid started. We all stayed in our seats after the announcement, until a thunderous crash brought us all to our feet. Then the power failed. Outside the cinema, white acrid smoke filled the street. Cries of 'Gas! Gas!' were heard. Mummy panicked and grabbed my hand as we ran this way, then that, to escape the choking fumes.

My gas-mask, in its battered box banging against my hip, never left me. I knew that the dismantled gas-mask was a sticky mess. I fumbled with it, while Mummy with her own in place was screaming weirdly through the mouth-piece. She pushed me against the wall frantically trying to get my mask over my head, but the strap snapped, the thing had rotted. She shook me, slapping me about the head. Then, ripping off her own mask, she tried to force it upon me. Refusing it, I ran with her, crouching through the cloud.

Of course it hadn't been 'GAS!' It had been a small chemical factory receiving a direct hit. Considering the fact that our eyes and throats were sticking and smarting for days after, Mummy's obvious relief was puzzling.

In order to avoid encountering people directly, I developed a habit of running everywhere. Somehow, I felt that people were judging me, observing my grubby, tatty clothes. Perhaps they even knew that I was a thief! Worse, I started to develop a mass of spots on my face – hives, which itched and became infected. Once, I'd leaned over the parapet and heard neighbours discussing us.

'That crazy woman . . . that child runs like a wild thing . . .

have you heard her speak? Like a lady . . . stole your milk for sure . . .!'

I raged. 'Bloody damn cheek! I never stole her smelly milk!'

It was true that I had long since left behind the Orphanage twang, adopting consciously Mummy's enunciation.

One day, after trotting through Kensington Gardens, I found myself in Exhibition Road, and came across the museums. Children and adults were going through the sand-bagged entrance. I tagged on behind a group of fresh-faced schoolgirls. The last two girls turned round and examined me briefly, tilting up their noses.

'Get that!' cried one, causing other girls to turn round.

'No thank you!' said the other, even louder.

'Sod the lot of you!' I spat out. Then, raising my elbows, I pulled my ears outwards and stuck out my long tongue and darted away.

Wandering through the porcelain department of the Victoria and Albert Museum, I was surprised by the exquisiteness of the objects in the china cabinets. The austere simplicity of line in the Chinese ware seemed to have an ethereal quality, a stillness, imparting a sense of tranquillity. Power and mass were the magic of the sleek Egyptian room, where I found the same essence of simplicity.

In my own palace, high in the hills of India where people would come to see me for wisdom . . . I would have this . . . this . . . and this, and I would arrange them so . . . and so . . .

A hand pulled me away from the cabinet. ''Op it!' A uniformed man pointed to the hallway. 'Go on, 'op it! Leaning on the glass like that! I'll say . . .!' he was muttering.

Imitating one of the nasty girls that I'd met in the entrance, I drew myself up and marched off. Perhaps I shouldn't have been in the porcelain rooms; nobody else was.

84

On my way home through the park, a little dog was running this way and that, yelping piteously. I called to it.

'You poor little thing! Is you lost then?' I stooped down and was immediately smothered in dog kisses. As I ran, the dog followed. I got tired and petted it again.

'Goodbye dog.'

Then I turned my back and walked off, but still the dog was behind me.

'I'm sorry, dog,' I said regretfully. 'You'll have to find someone else.' But he just put his head on one side and whimpered. 'You're ever so sweet.'

I had noticed an exceptionally well-dressed man watching me. He was now strolling over. As he neared, he raised his hat. I noticed that he was carrying gloves and a short cane; a military man, I thought.

'Excuse me, young lady, I do beg your pardon, but would, by any chance, that dog be for sale?'

'Could be.'

With some surprise, I felt myself blushing. I stopped just short of telling him that the dog wasn't mine.

He took out a ten-shilling note.

'I'd take great care of him.'

I eyed the note. The unaccustomed flush was still burning my cheeks, and I said, 'I don't know.'

'Oh, do forgive me!' He was putting the note away.

'You can have him,' I said decisively. 'We can't afford to feed him anyway.' And I pocketed the re-offered note and skipped off.

Once home, I pranced around as I told Mummy about the dog. She took the ten-shilling note and seemed delighted.

'Well I never, you monkey! Go and get me some cigarettes, love.' She tucked the note under her pillow and gave me some change.

'Oh Mummy, I'm so hungry!' I called to her from the kitchen.

'Well, get a bun then.' She gave me a few more coppers. 'Don't be long now,' she said, obviously desperate for a cigarette.

Pritchard's, the bread shop, was closed. I got the cigarettes and raced back. Mummy was standing against the wall of the sitting room awkwardly. She was staring straight ahead. I followed her gaze, but there was nothing exceptional to be seen.

'What's the matter, Mummy?'

She gave me a strange look. 'Where did you get this money from?'

She held out the screwed up note.

'I told you, Mummy, from that man who wanted the dog.'

'He gave you ten shillings for a stray dog?' She sounded antagonistic.

'Yes, Mummy, he did.'

'A soldier, you said?' She was looking terrifyingly angry.

'I didn't say he was a soldier, he wasn't in uniform. Why, Mummy? What's wrong?'

'Did he touch you?' Her eyes dilated.

'Touch me? Touch me? What for?' I couldn't understand what was upsetting her.

'You say this man gave you money in the park?' As she spoke she gave me a violent push. 'I want the truth out of you, my girl!' She started hitting out at me.

'You little whore! You dirty little tramp!'

Suddenly Mummy looked insane! The blows were breathtaking. I felt my whole body banged against the door-post as I tried to make my escape.

'Mummmeee, don't!' I screamed.

I managed to get to the kitchen. She attacked me again.

'Go on, Dorothy! Go on!'

She was calling me Dorothy! I ran desperately to the window, then sprang away from it in terror. I tried to dive past her, but she grabbed me. I saw the raised quart milk bottle . . .

Then I heard the tinkling of glass from a long way off. Slowly, like a chandelier gently waving in the breeze. I felt disembodied. I held on to the back of a chair to stop floating away. I felt sick. Mummy's white face was mouthing something. I strained my ears, but I couldn't hear her. A warmth trickled down the back of my neck; it felt good. I closed my eyes and felt my legs floating out behind me. I was slowly spinning flat out in the air. It was making me feel sick. My hands were hurting. Opening my eyes, I looked down and saw Mummy trying to prise them off the back of the chair. I wanted to tell her to leave them, but I couldn't speak, so I just watched her, feeling detached, as each finger was lifted.

In the doorway, I could make out Arthur, the old A.R.P. warden, the one who died, the one I'd loved.

'I'll take her,' he said gently.

'Feeling better?'

A nurse was bending over me searchingly.

'I've got a headache!' I said.

'Ah well, not too bad eh?' The nurse lifted my hand. It was very white. I meant to look at my other hand but I was too tired. Remembering everything, but pushing away the frights, I wanted to tell Mummy about the museum. I had to tell her! I closed my eyes.

'They say her mother did it!'

'My God!'

'How old is she?'

'We're not sure.'

I wanted to tell them I wasn't asleep, but I was too tired to open my eyes. They were whispering above me. 'We're not sure. . . .'

Mummy will get into trouble. Well I won't tell on her! I'll tell

87

them that I slipped on grease and the bottle fell on me and broke. Satisfied, I slept.

The sounds of hospital woke me. There was no one at my bedside now. Moving my head slowly, I found that it didn't hurt too much. I eased myself up and carefully looked about. Breakfast was being served from a trolley, no, it was only tea. I was asleep again before the trolley reached me. When I opened my eyes again, I saw everybody eating. Fearful that I would miss out I called to the nurse who rushed towards me.

'You're constipated!' said the sister, as she pulled up my nightie and examined my tummy. 'We'll do something about that. You can have something to eat now.'

Well, I don't fancy anything being done to my tummy, I thought, as I bolted my food.

Later in the day, two women came to my bedside, one with a writing pad.

'How are you, Marian? This is P.C. Smithers, and I'm a representative of the N.S.P.C.C., and we've come to help you.' I was on my guard. 'Tell us in your own words, as much as you can remember, what happened to you two days ago.'

Two days! My goodness!

'Well . . . I was in the kitchen and I fell, the floor was slippy or something . . . and this milk bottle . . . I must have knocked it . . . it smashed on my head.'

The two women exchanged glances. The one writing looked very severe as she pursed her lips. Did they believe me? I thought anxiously. The N.S.P.C.C. lady smiled, much to my relief.

'And where was your mother when this happened?'

'Oh, she was in bed . . . in her bedroom.' Oh dear! Suddenly my head was hurting.

'Come on, my dear, try to remember. The people underneath,

the wardens, they said they heard a lot of noise, they heard you screaming, would that be so? What were all the screams about?'

I clapped my hands to my head. 'I wasn't screaming, I was singing . . . I'm always singing . . . hymns and things. Oh yes, I screamed when I fell down, I remember that . . . and I cut myself, look!' I held out a bandaged arm.

'We don't think that's a cut,' the lady said quietly. 'You must tell us the truth if you want us to help you. You say this was an accident?'

'Oh yes!' I said, decisively grasping at the word. 'It was an accident!' I was feeling hot and my head was drumming. 'I want to see my mother! When can I see her?'

The sister came over and put her cool, cool hand on my forehead and picked up my hand. 'That's enough! Leave her now.'

The two ladies hesitated.

'We don't have very much!' said the policewoman.

'I'm sorry, but you must go now!' Sister was very firm, and the two walked away.

'I want to see my mother! I must see her!' I shouted.

'Come, come, visiting hours aren't here yet! You'll have to be patient like everyone else. I'll get something for that poor head of yours, all right?' She brought me a draught of something white and sweet, and soon I wandered off into sleep.

When I awoke it was pitch dark. For a while I wondered where I was, then I heard whisperings. Putting out my hand, I felt the curtains. They'd drawn them around my bed. It was night and I'd missed all the food. I felt like crying. They'd let me miss the lunch, the tea and the dinner. Maybe they'd even had supper, you always had a lot in institutions. I pushed the curtain back a little and made out the dim figures of two nurses writing and softly tittering with a candle burning between them.

'Nurse, nurse!' I called in a whisper.

A young nurse came over to me.

'Shush!' she said, and gently pushed me down, shoving a thermometer in my mouth.

'Did my mother come?'

'Now close your mouth and don't talk for a minute. Do you think you could manage that? You must be quiet, there are lots of very sick people here trying to sleep.' The nurse took the thermometer away, but returned in a moment.

'I didn't have my dinner!' I said querulously.

'Well, I'll see what I can find.' She went off and brought a cup of tea and two slices of bread and butter.

I tugged at her apron. 'Did my mother come?'

'I expect so. I really don't know. I'm on nights. Now be a good girl, as quiet as a mouse, eh?'

I had a lovely time at the hospital, with all the food I could wish for. Soon I was singing some of my favourite hymns and 'choruses'. I loved the melodies and I knew all the words, the more dramatic the better. I sang for the joy of the hymns, not for their religious content, although some of the ladies thought me 'a little angel'.

Mummy never came.

Although I longed to tell her that it was all right, that I hadn't betrayed her, I reasoned that she wouldn't like these people.

The stitches were removed, as well as the dressings and I gingerly felt the scabby bald patch. Showered with gifts of clothes and food, I was allowed to go home.

EIGHT

Fire

Halting on the stairs by the open door of the A.R.P. station, I poked my head in, whispering to the warden bending over a street map, 'Have you seen my mother? Is she all right?'

'Hey, you startled me!' Then he turned around to the others in the room. 'Look what we've got here!'

'Shush please!' I said fearfully, remembering that I was on forbidden territory.

'How come they let you come here?' He had lowered his voice.

Two of the other chaps appeared and one examined my head.

'Jesus!'

'Oh it's fine. It doesn't hurt a bit.'

'Tough littlen, ain't yer?' another said, looking me up and down. 'An' you look real nice in them clothes, quite the lady.'

I gave him a low curtsey, almost losing my balance.

'How's my mother? Have you seen her?'

'I guess she's all right.' The men exchanged glances. 'Shall I come up with you?'

'No, thank you.' I picked up my stuffed carrier bags.

'Now listen here, little Missy. You have any trouble with your mum an' you come straight down to us old codgers, right?'

I nodded.

Stamping hard upon the bare wooden stairs, I announced my presence, and heard Mummy cry out.

'Who's that?'

'It's me, Mummy, it's Marian,' I said brightly.

Mummy gave me a look of timorous apprehension. I dropped my bags and flung myself into her arms and we both wept.

'I thought they had taken you. It would have served me right. I just lay down to die!'

The two of us sobbed. But finding it impossible to sustain such a mood for long, I sprang back, pirouetted like I'd seen on the films and ended with a ballerina pose.

'And what do you think of your charming daughter, Mother dear?' Then I emptied the contents of the bags upon the table.

'What finery, to be sure!' said Mummy clasping her hands in exaggerated wonder.

Then we were laughing and chatting happily.

'I'll make you a cup of tea,' I said.

'Oh, I did miss your tea, my love.'

My happiness was supreme! Words like 'darling', 'my love', 'my sweet' trickled into my ears like honey, and I sang at the top of my voice as I made the tea.

> Mummy loves me this I know
> For I heard her tell me so
> To each other we belong
> She's always right
> And I'm never wrong
> Yes Mummy loves me . . . Yes Mummy loves me
> Yes Mummy loves me . . . I know . . . She told me so!

After a week at home, I awoke one morning with a terrible tummy ache. Not the usual hunger cramps, the pain was lower down and travelled down my legs. I'd always sprung out of bed, but this morning I could easily have lain there with my knees to my chin. Nevertheless, I forced myself up and drank some tea, and felt somewhat better. Perhaps the cigarette I'd smoked the night before, after Mummy had retired, was responsible. It had made me feel quite woozy and prickly, and I'd choked and spluttered in my efforts to master the art. I decided to go out and get some air.

I meant to go to the park, but the chill wind seemed to have directed my footsteps. In Whiteley's I felt the pain, still, like a dull ache. I hadn't been here since I'd been nabbed, and I was doubtful that they'd recognise me. I loved the central staircase in the store. Perhaps I'd even condescend to have it in my 'palace', I mused, as I ascended the slow spiral.

Suddenly I noticed blood on my sock, it was on my leg too! The stain in Mummy's bed flashed before me. Terror gripped me. Perhaps I was dying. Running down the stairs, I stood in an alcove of suitcases, hiding my tears. Then I remembered something. 'Constipated!' that's what the sister had said. The sister had said that they'd do something about it and they never did.

Ever practical, I went to the hospital, straight to 'my' ward, and sought out a familiar face among the nurses.

'What are you doing here?' The nurse showed concern. 'Not your mother again?'

'No! I'm bleeding, I've got a pain here.' I swept my hand over my lower tummy. 'I think I've got Constipated!'

The nurse smiled. 'Have you now?' But she was examining my head. 'Well that's doing nicely. Where did you get the idea you were constipated?' She was grinning, then she sighed.

'You know you can't come trotting up here any time you like, bringing all sorts of germs with you!'

Surprised at her lack of concern, I persisted. 'I'm bleeding with it!'

The nurse chuckled. 'Don't you know anything?' Then she

sighed again. 'I'm frightfully busy, but come on, I'll take you to the lady almoner, she'll set you straight!'

'Please help me.'

The nurse took both my hands. 'Look, what is happening is perfectly natural. You've nothing to fear, you're all right, see?'

Marching after her, I went down the stairs and into a small office. We entered after a perfunctory knock at the door.

'Mrs Soams, I have this child here with her first period. She knows positively nothing. She thinks she's dying of constipation. She was a patient in our ward with a head fracture, under circumstances we were not happy about. Please could you sort it out for her?' She turned to me. 'All right? Mrs Soams is just the person to help you. She's a genius!' and the nurse bolted.

Mrs Soams came around the desk and looked at my head. 'Do you get any pain, any headaches?'

'No.'

After telling her my name and that I was nearly twelve, and answering all the usual questions, I was given the extraordinary explanation of my bleeding, followed by a definition of constipation. Then I was given a packet of enormous maternity sanitary towels, five shillings and a promise I could come and see Mrs Soams again. Somehow I knew I just wouldn't.

Half running home, and feeling unhappy at the unbelievable prospect of bleeding once a month for what seemed forever, I became aware of the great sanitary towel that chafed between my legs like sandpaper. Finally, it became so painful that I fished it out of my knickers and stuffed it down my dress. I couldn't tolerate the thing another step.

Mummy was pottering about the kitchen.

A little nervously, I plonked the parcel and the five shillings on the table.

'I was given that at the hospital,' I said quickly to deflect any

94

possible doubts that she might have over the money. 'I've got my period!'

Mummy patted me sorrowfully. 'Well, you're almost grown up,' and then she laughed over the size of the packet. 'Come on, love, we'll get you tiddler towels for tiny tots!'

And after Mummy threw on her clothes, off we went.

When we returned, a letter addressed to me was stuck in the board in the hallway. It was my very first letter, and it was from Millicent with a postal order for my birthday.

Snatching the letter from me, Mummy pored avidly over the contents. Then she screwed it up and threw it down, immediately retiring to her bed.

Retrieving the letter and reading the contents, I was happy that Millicent was working. She'd been in touch with Dorothy, was sorry about Anthony, and she hoped I'd mend my ways and that the letter would reach me. Nothing else, and no address.

For a month Mummy stayed in her bed.

I would provide her with tea and empty the two-pound jam jars of urine. Sometimes she would not allow me to empty them. She wished to compare the varying amounts of blood they contained over a period of days. And then I would be sent out to find more jam jars.

She had to have cigarettes, tea, sugar and milk. These I would steal, along with whatever I could find to keep hunger at bay. Sadly, I stole milk from the A.R.P. men. I felt really mean. I found I just couldn't beg any more. I became self-conscious, and even shy. Dorothy was right, begging was the lowest step on the ladder.

Mummy had that pasty look again. She would often have conversations with invisible people, looking wild as she sat cross-legged among the stinking jam jars. I was terrified that she might come and kill me in the night, so I'd sleep close to the

95

wall, under my bed. In the daytime, apart from seeing to her basic needs, I would avoid her.

I discovered the Natural History and Science Museums. I'd spend most of my days stuck up against the glass cabinets, moving off only when crowds of schoolchildren carelessly invaded the halls, racing about, and seeming to show not the slightest interest in the displays. I loathed them and their intrusion. In fact, I didn't like people much at all. Inevitably, they would look me up and down rudely, and I would stare defiantly back at them. 'Puddings! A damned lot of bloody puddings!' I'd say courageously when they had gone.

It was almost June and Mummy began to get better; she was eating a little. The foul jars disappeared and a washing of clothes and a great clean-up brought chat and laughter between us.

'Come, my girl. I want you to put your nicest things on. We're going on the town.'

Mummy got dressed in her black and white polka-dot dress with the swinging skirt. She wore her fine black straw hat with the large brim, straight on her head, and pulled the veil over her face and pulled on her long black gloves. I placed her dark fur stole over her shoulders. Although she was pale and thin, she looked beautiful in my eyes.

We took the bus up to the West End. Soon we were sitting on gilt chairs in a smart restaurant, surrounded by elegant elderly people and a couple of middle-aged soldiers arguing noisily over Allied tactics. A young couple, both in uniform, were silent and seemed sad. They hardly spoke. He toyed with her little finger, while with her free hand she just picked at her food.

An array of cutlery was laid out before me. A tiny posy in a pretty glass vase next to an unlit candle and a little basket of bread were in the centre of the table. I ran my fingers over the stiff white table cloth. It was so beautifully clean. I followed

Mummy's example and placed the even stiffer napkin on my lap.

We started with a delicate soup, followed by pease pudding, cabbage and the sweetest boiled carrots. A delicious ice-cold blancmange followed.

Then Mummy leaned over me.

'Now, my love, I've lost my purse! See?' I smiled gleefully. 'No, keep a straight face. Act unconcerned!' Then a last look and, 'Sit up straight, remember, you're a young lady.'

She snapped her fingers imperiously and demanded the bill. The smarmy waiter minced over and placed it on the table. Mummy went through the motions of looking for her purse. She demanded to see the manager, who seemed a charming fellow.

'I must have had it. I must have paid the taxi-driver!' she said, as she delved through her handbag.

'No, I did, Mother! But I'm afraid I haven't a penny left!' Then I gave a look of studied remembrance. 'Oh, I do remember, Mother! I'm afraid the whole thing's my fault. I paid that chap for the thing-a-me-bob . . . I left your purse on the hall table. I say, Mother! How will we get home?'

I saw a glint of warning in Mummy's eye, so I left it at that.

The manager took out his own wallet and left a ten shilling note on the table.

'Allow me?' was all he said. He didn't even ask us to pay the bill later.

Outside, we made a show of gesticulating wildly for a taxi and then sped round a corner doubling up with laughter.

'Mother dear, do you really think we should have done that?' I said in the bla-bla tones of a 'lady'!

We repeated this drama many times, although not all the managers were as charming as the first one. Often they were abusive and threatened police action and we had to run for it.

Sometimes I was left for surety, but I would always make my escape with relative ease.

Food restored Mummy's health. I dragged her around the museums and told her about the palace of my dreams.

'You're a funny little thing,' she said affectionately. 'If you don't end up in the gutter, you just might make that palace!'

But Mummy found the museums tedious, and these visits ended.

A letter arrived from George.

I didn't care for the idea of him, nor Mummy's slushy attitude in the way she'd clasped the letter to her and rushed into the bedroom to read it, all on her own.

'George is sending me thirty pounds!'

She waved the letter at me as I stood at the open door. Then she kissed it. 'Oh you darling man! We'll go on holiday, perhaps to the seaside.' Then, aware of my misery, she added, 'Oh come on, you'll like my George, why don't you write him a nice letter?'

I stiffened, 'What am I supposed to call him then?'

'You can call him "Daddy"!'

Sulkily I turned my head away.

'Oh call him anything you like, but don't mess it up for me!' She held out the letter. 'It's my last chance for happiness!'

'Oh Mummy, I'm such a pig! I'll write to him today!'

Hardly knowing what to say, I cheated, taking up most of the paper with a drawing of a little girl standing on tiptoes kissing an airman. Mummy was delighted and showed me some exquisite drawings she had done many years ago. She told me that she had met George briefly before the war, and that they had married just before he had embarked on overseas service.

The money arrived and we set off for the seaside. We stayed in a room on the first floor of a narrow Georgian house. Renting a hut on the beach, we went shrimping with huge nets, played ball, built sandcastles and did all the things one has to do at the seaside.

Several times we sat on a rock in the magnificent spray and shouted to the elements, laughing and screaming, but the wind snatched away our voices, so that we heard not a whisper from each other. We returned to the beach hut like a couple of drowned rats, in a state of happy exhaustion. So the days were spent, happily, extravagantly, and at times magically.

On the last night, she sent me to bed early, while she went to the cinema. I idly listened to the landlady's drunken return, whooping and singing as she slammed the doors below. Mummy had more than once argued with her about her swearing and filthy language, protesting at the innocence of her little girl. Often in the morning the landlady, looking somewhat delicate, would be oh so genteel. She would lift her little finger over her cup of tea in the breakfast room, and look down her nose at the manners of the family who had the rooms above us. So musing, I fell asleep.

Suddenly I was awake! Smoke! I sat up and sniffed the air, switching on the light with the pull switch above my head. I saw the smoke creeping and swirling from under the door. My whole body quickened and my hair prickled as I made a dash for the door. Then I turned to see that Mummy had not been lying next to me.

As I opened the door, I was immediately aware of a great roar. The stifling smoke was rushing up the stairs at a tremendous rate! Without thinking, I dashed upstairs to the family above, banged frantically on their door and shouted, 'Fire! Fire!' Then turned and raced downstairs barefoot in my nightie.

Instantly, there was a mighty thunderous splitting and crashing! Then a terrifying rush as the flames exploded up the stairs, but I ran through them and out of the front door which had blown out.

It was as if my feet never touched the stairs. My long blonde hair was dirtied, but only my eyebrows were singed. It had been a race that I would run again and again, for many years to come, in my dreams.

Mummy had arrived just as the house had gone up in flames. Several people were holding her down on the ground while she screamed and thrashed about. I ran to her and flung myself beside her. She clasped me savagely to her.

Then the fire-engines arrived and we were whipped away by a nice couple. Later we heard that the family had got out intact, but that the landlady had met her end.

We'd lost everything in about thirty seconds. Our clothes and (ahem!) the rest of the one hundred pounds from 'Daddy', also (little cough!) our ration books and goodness knows what. In the war, so many had lost so much, but not in this sleepy seaside town. Wonderful people raised nearly fifteen pounds for us, and nice clothes for me and 'mingy cast-offs' for Mummy. Local authorities provided us with two pounds, travel vouchers, and temporary ration documents. People showered us with gifts, home-made cakes and even soap, as if we had been burned out of our own home.

The travel documents weren't used. A group of American soldiers adopted us and we accompanied them in their coach, all the way to London. We sang and sang! I learned 'Peg o'my heart, I love you!' and 'There's just one place for me, near you!', and sang all by myself.

Half a dozen of the soldiers trooped out of the coach, which had made a special detour, dropping us near the flat. They carried our bags up the stairs and loaded us with more gifts and money. They kissed Mummy on the lips, me on top of my head, and made a noisy, happy exit down the stairs.

I was given a beautiful new gas-mask. We got new ration books (the first I'd ever seen), and more money from some authority.

So we passed the rest of the summer.

One day, in Oxford Street, I bumped into Dorothy. She looked quite a lady, all grown up with her pretty hair in a rather severe roll around the back of her head. I was amazed to see that she had bosoms, but I pretended not to notice. She had forsaken her steel-rimmed glasses, of which I'd been quite fond, for horrid flesh-coloured pink things, sort of butterfly shaped, which somehow didn't go with the taut hairstyle.

I nearly cried with joy at seeing her.

She told me that she was now training seriously in a hospital somewhere in the country. She didn't seem a bit pleased to see me, in fact she lectured me, saying that Anthony's trouble was all my fault.

I stood miserably, while Dorothy had to rush.

I'd had so much to tell her! I didn't believe that Dorothy could think so harshly of me. Surely I wasn't that wicked? I looked wistfully after her as she rapidly disappeared at a determined pace, which I knew would stand her in good stead.

On the way home, I thought about Dorothy. The two of us were so different. She had an intensity about her, a desperation that drove some of the joy of life away from her. Yet she had a great capacity for humour. I sighed to myself, sadly realising that Dorothy had dismissed me, leaving me with the vague notion that she carried little hope for me and perhaps no longer cared for me. Yet I was already aware that Dorothy needed to give all her attention to her own life, in order to escape the possibility of falling back into the life of insecurity with me and Mummy. 'Well, I guess I am wicked!' I thought. 'It's true I made Anthony steal. Yet she used to love me. She used to call me "My little sister"!'

Fortunately, I had a way of throwing unpleasant thoughts out of my mind. I wiped my stinging eyes. Before long I was whizzing through the streets, darting nimbly around solid citizens,

and making a point of not stepping on any join in the pavement
as if my life depended on it, each crack a chasm into hell.

NINE

Damnation

By the end of September Mummy was ill again, and the jam jar routine was begun again. This time it was evident that her condition was more serious. When I suggested that she should go to hospital, she leapt up from her bed, and I shot out of the flat and down the stairs.

'God strike you dead!', 'You'll not put me away!' and 'Over my dead body!' I heard her yelling still from the street.

My immediate thought was food. Cigarettes and food! For weeks now we hadn't had a proper meal and for at least two days we'd had nothing at all. The day before I just managed to grab a packet of tea and had to make a dash out of the shop, leaving a commotion behind. I ran to the hidy-hole that had been a secret between Anthony and me. I was a shivering, shattered mess!

Now today, stealing would have been as easy as pie, but somehow I fluffed it and moved guiltily away with nothing. Indeed, in some of my usual haunts I had the feeling that I was being watched. Pushing away the thought that I had lost my nerve, I went further afield, and found myself just off Baker Street.

It was now dark. The shops had closed and very few people were moving about. Feeling defeated and unable to go home without at least the cigarettes, I sat upon the steps of an elegant house with my head cradled between my arms. After a few minutes of inactivity I began to feel cold and was about to move off, when I heard someone with light steps approaching. The moon was full and bright. A little old lady drew near. As she passed, I was suddenly mesmerised by a glint of light reflected from the clasp on her handbag.

The tiny light drew my eyes as it briefly flashed through the railings, then disappeared. Swiftly rising, I silently darted after her and grabbed at her bag. Immediately she let out ear-piercing screams, one after the other. With incredible strength she clung to her bag. Then she lost her balance and I saw her face, like a little round disc of moonlight. A mask of toothless terror screaming! I let go in horror, turned and ran, the shrill cries pursuing me.

Then I heard the urgent, dull thuds of heavy steps behind me. I ran on desperately, frantically trying to evade the threat that was following me. The thundering footsteps were closing in. I knew that I could run no further, so I tumbled down some basement steps, crouching like a dog for the inevitable capture.

A large hand grabbed me by the hair and hauled me up the steps. I was held in mid-air and thumped until the breath went out of me. Then I was being dragged at a great pace along the pavement. I struggled to find a footing. I knew the old lady was following, for I heard her cry out: 'Oh God!' and 'Please don't!'

Inside the police station I was thrown on to a bench. I was a mass of pain, and hardly able to breathe. People around me were shouting, the old lady protesting. Someone was asking my name but I saw only that little round disc in the moonlight and felt utterly damned!

The old lady was being reprimanded for refusing to make charges against me. I wished she would! I saw her tiny pointed buttoned boots as she stood for a moment in front of me, but I couldn't raise my head. I'd never be able to lift up my head again!

A policeman picked me up and placed me upon a bed in a cell. To his enquiries, I whispered my name and address and that I wanted nothing. Then I was left alone, but the cell door was left open. I sat with my arms clasped around my knees, slowly rocking myself to and fro. It seemed I stayed for hours like that, just rocking backwards and forwards, trying to blot out my mind.

A man's voice said: 'That kid's crazy, just like her mother!'

I let out a wail, for I knew it to be true! I felt diminished, broken and destroyed, and I'd done it myself. I prayed that I might die. Perhaps I was in the middle of a bad dream and that the little round disk would go back to the moon. Perhaps I was an illusion.

A kind, burly policeman was standing over me with a mug of tea. I must have slept. Someone had covered me with a blanket. I was so stiff and in such pain that I could hardly move, but finally I put out a dirty hand for the tea.

'You're in a right mess, aren't you?' he said, gently.

I sniffed and wobbled up upon my haunches.

'You're to see the doctor soon.'

I leaned away, 'Oh no! No!' Then the memories came flooding back and I turned away from him in shame.

'You need to see him, Miss. You fell down those steps, you remember?'

'Yes . . . and he punched me . . . that man punched me!'

'Now, now, you're making that up, aren't you?' He sounded surprised, and then added: 'It won't do you any good to say things like that!'

I said nothing. It didn't matter anyway. It was punishment!

'I want to see my mother.'

'Tell us about her.'

'She's sick and she needs me.' I was suddenly anxious about her. 'Does she know about me?'

'Yes, we've seen her all right, and she don't need you and you don't need her. She wants you taken care of and that's what's going to happen.'

My legs started to tremble on their own and I had a fearsome headache. I couldn't make out what he was saying.

'Now you lay there quiet see?' And he went off.

The next thing I remember was being lifted up into sturdy arms, with the blanket drawn about me, and deposited into a car. Later we swept into the drive of a large house where I was again carried up the steps and sat on a bench in the hallway. Immediately I was taken to a room and stripped. I stood, hanging my head, naked and trembling.

Then I felt hands going all over me. Someone was examining me with quick deft movements. I was lifted into a bath filled with deep, blue, hot water, which eased the stiffness.

'What a sight we are! We have been in the wars, haven't we?' The voice was brisk, but it got no response. She remained quiet as she draped a large towel around me, guided me towards a desk, and gently placed me on a chair.

'Well, what have we here?'

A lady doctor had been sitting there all the time.

I thought for a moment and said, 'Nothing.'

· The doctor sounded surprised. 'Nothing? That's a funny thing to say, isn't it?' There was a tinge of amusement in her voice. 'You can't be nothing, can you?'

'I am nothing!' I said firmly.

'Oh dear! Is it as bad as all that?' she moved round the desk. 'Well I don't often have the opportunity to examine nothing at all! Will you stand?'

There followed a fairly intensive examination. Then she applied stinging lotion to various injuries, which I received without flinching. Still hanging my head, I noticed a large bruise spreading across my chest. I thought of the man punching me and I saw the little white disk in the moonlight again. I felt faint and was bundled into bed.

A hand tugged at the sheet. I awoke and was given a bowl of bread and milk. At first I felt that I couldn't eat, but I soon gulped it down and felt a glow of warmth. My trembling legs quieted and once again I fell asleep.

It was dusk when more food was brought: a veritable feast. The nurse said that I was to have a mixture of cod liver oil and malt. This sounded revolting, like fish guts. I hesitated while the spoon which held the thick, sticky, brown mass was twirled above me, threatening to spill, and I was forced to accept it.

Already feeling better, I became aware that I was in a dimly lit room with five other beds. The sound of girls singing hymns downstairs made me think that I was in a remand centre. Later I heard the girls getting into their beds. Unable to face them, I pretended to be asleep.

Throughout the night, the girl in the next bed sobbed and often called out piteously, 'Oh Gran! Oh Gran!'

Poor thing! I thought. Yet I viewed with apprehension the loathsome idea that I was in the company of other girls. Thoughts came rushing into my head. Mummy didn't, couldn't, want me any more! I heard the policeman saying, 'She don't need you' and 'She wants you taken care of.' I felt a warmth and pulsing in my throat. Dorothy was right! I had let the devil take hold of me. A vision of my good, kind sister flashed before my eyes, then disappeared. I wanted to ask her what to do, which way to the bottomless pit? To oblivion? Then the sobs rolled over me and I called out. 'Do . . . ro . . . thy!'

There was no Dorothy to say 'my little sister' so prettily to me, and I wasn't dreaming. I sat up, clasped my knees and started rocking. 'Maybe I am crazy?' I said to myself. 'Mad like Mummy? Daddy Jim killed himself, that was horribly mad! I am bad! . . . Mad! . . . Sad!' Flinging myself back on the bed, bathed in dreadful remorse, I curled myself into a ball and covered my head with the sheets.

It was not a remand centre but some kind of temporary home for war-shattered girls. The little girl in the bed next to me had lost her grandmother, mother, aunt, two sisters and a baby brother with one bomb. Another had been buried with her mother and they'd held hands for many hours while the mother had slowly died. I felt humbled by such tales. I'd lost no one, except perhaps myself, and I'd been blubbing over my own insignificance. Somewhere I'd heard the song: 'You pick yourself up and you start all over again!'

My misery dissipated and up bubbled my cheerful self. Throwing out my sins and tucking them away in a dark corner, I thought only of breakfast, lunch, dinner and tea, perhaps even supper too! These wishes were soon realised and before long I was to be 'sessed, as one girl called it.

'Now, Marian, we have to find out what to do with you!' The nice doctor was smiling. 'Tell us about yourself.'

'I'm Welsh!' I announced to her evident surprise.

'Welsh?' she said, quizzically surveying her notes.

'Yes, Welsh! My father was a miner in Wales!' I wished I could speak in the sing-song manner of the inhabitants of Symonds Yat.

'Your mother is English?'

'Well, sort of. She's really half an Indian princess!' I watched the doctor's eyes widen.

'Well! From being "nothing", we're now elevated to royalty! We have come a long way.' I wished I hadn't said it. The doctor carried on. 'Well, let's get a few mundane facts right, shall we? How old are you?'

'Twelve,' I answered sheepishly.

'And you have two sisters and a brother. Is that right?' I nodded. 'You have a stepfather?'

'He's not my father!' I examined my feet.

'Perhaps he'd like to be? Have you thought about that?'

'No. I haven't thought about that. I've never seen him. He's never seen me! I don't think he'd want me.'

'He might, you know. I think he well might. You look quite different from a week ago. You're capable and helpful, you're also a kind little girl. You've made a good impression here.' I felt my face reddening. 'We thought of fostering you out to a family in the country. Would you like that?'

'In Wales?'

'I think, I can't absolutely promise, that we can arrange that. Oh and there's something else. I thought you'd like to know that we've been in touch with the Revd McCann.'

I'd not heard of him, I told her.

She explained that the Revd McCann was the director of the N.S.P.C.C., who'd been in touch with my sisters and brother. Millicent and Dorothy were happy and well. Anthony was doing forestry work. I could just picture him. Oh that was good. Dear Anthony!

'Now run along. You'll be here for a few weeks yet. I'll give you a few days' warning before you leave us.'

The weeks were spent in kindly company. Even the girls were unexpectedly pleasant. There were those I called 'my poor things'. I would prance around them, fuss over them, and tell stories that might make them laugh.

Scrubbing and cleaning would be done to the best of my ability, for this was the only way I cared to approach any task. My efficiency surprised the staff who would pat and praise me, and I'd lap it all up a little shyly.

Now almost fit, my tremendous energy seemed to overflow and I'd have outbursts of singing. I'd sing hymns or the few popular songs that I knew, much to everyone's amusement.

One insistent little girl would thrust under my nose a terrible comic book, shake my arms and point to the page. She wanted the same awful story again and again. The little girl hadn't spoken a word since being picked out of the rubble of a house. I tried to make her speak by saying the wrong words, for I was sure she knew them off by heart. But all I got from her was a shove or a pinch. Every day she bothered me with that book but I hadn't the heart to refuse her.

One day the doctor called me.

'Your transport will be here in a couple of days. Yes, Wales it is! In case I don't have time for a chat, I want to tell you that it's been a pleasure to have you here.' With that, she stooped and kissed the top of my head and was gone.

'Ten minutes Marian!'

Wildly excited, I looked forward to the coach journey and the inevitable sing-songs. I raced upstairs to say goodbye to everyone and kiss 'my poor little things' and then waited with Cook in the biting wind.

Unexpectedly, a large black car drew up and an ample lady alighted from the front, shouting in a deep plummy voice to the driver. He picked up my brown paper bags and I noticed the elegant cases that were strapped to the roof.

A kiss from Cook, and I piled into the back of the car where three little boys with fat white knees in light grey school uniform made room for me. Then I turned and waved frantically to Cook and saw the little girl holding out the comic book.

She was shouting and crying as Cook picked her up in her arms: 'Who'll read me? Who'll read me?'

TEN

Wales

'Come on, Miss.' The driver spoke politely as he closed the door.

I squeezed between the boys and saw their little putty hands. As I lifted my head and saw their faces I nearly burst out laughing. With their little snouts, widely spaced tiny pale blue eyes and stubbly blond hair, they looked like the three little pigs in the story. Two were a pair and the little one looked identical, apart from his size. To my relief, they were all smaller than myself.

For a while, I contented myself in the appraisal of the enormous car. Very swish! I thought. Soon we were purring out of London, picking up speed and racing through the countryside. For a long time not a word passed between us.

'My name's Marian!' I announced to the smallest piggy. But he cast his eyes up to heaven and kept quiet.

Slyly, I tried again. 'You must be the eldest.'

'He's the youngest,' the other two said, both together, and then proved that they could rattle on ten times faster than I could. They were very quarrelsome, too, so that I began to wish I'd kept quiet.

They had been named Peter, Paul and James. 'Just James' the older boys called the little one as if he was a flea or something. James's voice sounded like the whine of a mosquito, and more than once I had to resist the temptation to swat him as he constantly tugged at me querulously, to make sure that I listened to him.

They had just come back from America where their mother had sent them, but she was pining to death and had bought a country mansion where she was waiting for them. The lady with the chauffeur was from 'the agency'. Somehow I was relieved. I liked her powerful, extravagant air and had been feeling sorry for her as the mother of these three.

About half way through our journey, we pulled into the drive of a fine house where we were to have a meal. The little piggies tumbled out, having pushed me aside, when two large, ferocious dogs leapt at them. The piggies quickly retreated, diving behind me. I found the dogs terrifying, but slowly and, I hoped, with the greatest of dignity, I alighted from the car. The two dogs whipped past me, snarling and barking through the open car door, barring the little boys' attempts to follow me. The boys' howls mingled with those of the dogs.

'Put those dogs under control!' demanded the agency lady imperiously.

A slight young woman called to them: 'Pride, come here! Come here!' Astonishingly they obeyed her. 'Get!' She pointed to a gateway, and they meekly scampered through, and remained looking through the open gate.

The boys joined me, and we were presented to the young woman who solemnly shook hands with us.

Hand-embroidered linen place-mats were positioned underneath finely decorated cream dinner-plates. Heavily embossed silver cutlery matched the imposing candelabra. An enormous display of heavy-odoured white chrysanthemums adorned the centre of the highly polished dinner table.

A butler with peculiarly staring eyes brought in trays, from which a very young girl in a neat uniform nervously unloaded and precariously placed tureens upon the central mats.

A thin soup was served, to which was added little bits of toast (which I thought rather odd). Potatoes, parsnips, cauliflower, grilled tomatoes and meat rissoles. (I was grateful to see more carrot than meat.) Little dishes of white sauce and another of green sauce and a jug of brown gravy were offered. Great piles of crisp lettuce and jugs of celery gave an air of opulence. This banquet was followed by a fresh fruit salad.

The stay was brief, but it made an immense impression on me. The soft crunch of the car tyres along the sweeping driveway banked by rolling lawns, bushes and trees; the many-roofed rambling house covered in luxuriant flame-leaved growth; curtains and furniture covers in flowered chintz; the polished dining table streaked with sunlight; the fine china and silver service with cloth napkins; and most of all the air of polite, if a little distant, civility and unassuming self-assured affluence that cloaked the inhabitants in gracious calm.

All too soon we were back on the road, where we swept over hills and dales towards the mansion of the pining mother. At the end of an isolated bleak village, we stopped in front of a tiny chapel. The agency lady rang the visitor's bell and helped me out of the car, depositing my paper bags upon the ground.

'Thank you ever so much,' said the vicar, a thin blue-nosed figure shaking in the wind.

The lady shook my hand vigorously while looking at the vicar. 'Not at all! We all have to do our bit!'

I waved goodbye a trifle sadly at the three little piggies and the prospect of their elegant mansion.

'Come, my dear, Mrs Withers, my housekeeper, will make tea. Then I'll take you over to Mrs Jones. You were to go to her sister, but at the last minute, only this afternoon, in fact, they realised that there was nowhere for you to sleep. Mrs Jones said she'll be glad to have you.'

It all seemed a bit muddled, I thought, as I followed him into his freezing cold and dark cottage next to the chapel. Mrs Withers brought us incredibly strong tea, homemade bread, jam and cakes. She stood silently watching me as I grabbed the food, clucking with her head on one side while the vicar noisily drank the tea only, while reading a prayer book.

'Are you chapel or church?' he asked as we walked through the village which consisted of just two rows of dark stone slate-roofed buildings.

'Chapel,' I said, for no special reason, as we went on to the last house.

First knocking at the door, the vicar lifted the latch and called out. 'Mrs Jones! Mrs Jones!' then he turned to me. 'She's a mite deaf!'

We went directly into a large kitchen with a scrubbed white table and a long fitted dresser. Many chairs were drawn around a big black range where a black cauldron was steaming next to a large soot-covered kettle. We went on, through the scullery to the back door, which opened on to a partially covered yard. I followed the vicar down the garden to an array of rickety sheds. Mrs Jones was nowhere to be seen. We made our way back to the house and saw, against the back wall, an assortment of neatly stacked buckets and bowls underneath a long, rough, high table. Two zinc baths hung on the wall. Everything about the place was neat and clean.

Between the kitchen-cum-dining-room and the scullery, there was an alcove full of big coats and, beneath, a rack holding enormous polished boots. Here there was a door leading to a staircase and another leading to a parlour, only they didn't use it as a parlour, the vicar informed me. Then Mrs Jones came through the door.

'It's you, vicar, is it?' She looked me up and down. 'She's wee, ent she? Ten and six a week in the hand, is it?'

The vicar nodded and departed with a 'God bless you'.

Mrs Jones was thin and tired-looking, quite old too, I thought. She had large black eyes above high cheekbones, and a mop of iron-grey hair. Her gnarled red hands and long arms waved about her as she spoke.

'We don't stand on ceremony here, you'll be wanting the school?'

I shook my head vigorously. 'No!'

'Waste of time, is it?' Then she firmly held me at arms' length and looked me up and down. 'You do right with me and I'll be fair with you, is it?'

I nodded.

She took me upstairs and showed me my bed in 'Gran's room'. The old lady was in her own bed and smiled delightedly at seeing me.

'Come, child.' Gran opened her arms and I politely obliged. Looking and smelling as if she had just been scrubbed, her pink scalp showing through her pure white hair, she cuddled me as if I were a stray lamb.

Everything about her seemed trimmed with fine white lace, her nightie and the sheets, which were covered with a spotless white embroidered coverlet. The windows were also hung with lace. Lace draped from the high mantelpiece, below which a small fire burned in a tiny grate.

'You'll sleep on the cot. You won't mind an old woman, will you?' Gran said as she laughingly pinched my cheek.

I had thought of miners' homes as poor, and dirty with all the coal dust, but this house was ordered and gleaming. It soon became apparent that Mrs Jones spent her life cooking, cleaning, washing and ironing. She took the greatest care of her mother-in-law out of respect for her adored husband who had died in a pit accident many years previously.

Mrs Jones had four sons and a waif, a lad she'd taken in, who'd lost his father and elder brothers in the same incident that had deprived her of the love of her life. The boy's mother had died of a broken heart. All this was told to me by Gran. Mrs Jones rarely spoke and never smiled. Mostly she just pointed and grunted, but my intuitive nature quickly realised her demands.

'The men', as the great louts were called, would come home noisily the back way. Whatever the weather, they'd strip off everything, and wash down in the bowls of hot water Mrs Jones and I would strenuously provide for them. They never made any attempt to help with buckets being filled at the pump or with the great hods of coal we heaved about the house.

Each one of them would place a hand, black with coal dust upon my head, roughing up my blonde hair, making it filthy for the fun of it. I would duck through them, giving out towels, while, with coarse laughter, they would pull down their trousers and push me about with their bare bottoms.

After they had cleaned themselves, Mrs Jones and I would feed them and wait upon them. Then they'd stretch out by the fire reading bits of the one newspaper. There was no conversation around the fire, only grunts. Making no effort to be tidy, they would throw bits and pieces around. I was surprised that Mrs Jones didn't protest. Occasionally when a sheet of newspaper fell to the floor, one of the boys would sit up, make some kind of animal noise and point to it expecting me to pick it up. Needless to say, I never would!

When they had some money, they'd go to the pub. If they got drunk, they were not allowed into the house and would have no billy-can awaiting them at the crack of dawn.

I resented their attitude towards us. They showed no awareness of the hard grind the seven-days-a-week entailed for their mother, who also took care of Gran and another old biddy a few doors away.

Once I tried to talk to Mrs Jones, but she just sighed.

'They're only men, pack horses, but they bring the money home. You've got to give them their due.'

I realised with astonishment that she despised them, her own sons.

'Not all men are like that!' I said, thinking of my beloved A.R.P. men. They'd been sensitive and kind, and once Anthony and I had followed them and saw how they treasured the life of a woman.

'Show me one, just one?' Then she gazed wistfully ahead, dropping her long arms and looking a picture of sorrow. 'There was one, he'd not let me carry the heavy'uns, but the Lord took him!'

There was no joy in the household except for Gran. Even she was rather keen on the old hell-and-damnation stuff. My singing amused her and she'd say it was my Welsh soul that couldn't abide foreign parts that drove me to it. She was ungrateful to her daughter-in-law and hadn't seen 'those downstairs' for years. But she was sweet to me. She'd cackle and neigh when I told her stories of the Orphanage and the goings-on with the war in London.

I told her my mother was dead, and she'd hug me and I'd weep a little for what I'd lost.

One morning, still dark, I was woken, as was usual, by the men leaving and the other general noise of the miners calling to each other. They sounded happy, and laughed and joked as they passed our house on the way to the mine which lay beyond the village. Usually Gran would call out to me, but I learned to pretend to be asleep, gaining a couple more hours in bed.

This morning, she didn't call to me and it was light when I arose. I found Gran lying on her back, motionless, her mouth like a little round hole and her eyes blankly staring. I approached her warily. She was not breathing. I hesitantly picked up her hand. It was ice cold and felt solid.

Gran was dead!

For a moment I just stood there looking at her, not feeling anything much. I totally accepted the demise of the old lady. Then I turned and dashed down the stairs and out into the yard where I heard the swish-swish of Mrs Jones sweeping. I tiptoed to her in my bare feet and tugged at her arm. Mrs Jones just looked at me as I stood panting, gasping in the cold air, not able to think of the right words.

'You get dressed and get Dr Foster,' she said as she put the broom under cover in a slow deliberate manner. I'd said nothing, but she knew! She didn't seem the least bit sad; she was calm and immensely practical. I dashed up the stairs ahead of her for I was freezing, and had quickly dressed, skipping the usual wash in the enamelled basin, before Mrs Jones had reached the room.

Mrs Jones just stood looking at Gran for a moment, then said, 'You'd better pack up your things, you won't want to sleep here,' quite without emotion, 'but first get the doctor.'

I ran to the doctor's house on the other side of the village. When I returned I saw a small congregation of women looking immensely cheerful outside. They made way for me. Upstairs two women were hovering over Gran's body. I was invited to observe the practice of laying-out. I declined and proceeded to pack my few possessions.

It was while I was thus occupied that I began to think that the cheerless atmosphere would be intolerable without Gran to chat to, to sing to. Gran had been affectionate, had called me a 'strange one sent to bring a ray of sunshine' to her life, and other pretty things. It was not that I regretted Gran dying; poor Gran was riddled with painful twisted joints, so her death was a blessed relief. But I felt the sudden loss of animated conversation.

Gran would support her great bosoms and laugh like a donkey, causing me to fall about in uncontrollable giggles. She had such tales to tell me of the mines, the hardships and deprivation suffered by the men in the strikes. Unaware of it at the time, I had had from Gran my first lesson in economics.

In the two months I'd been here I'd acquired nothing new.

Almost without thinking, I was discarding this and that as being not worth carrying. Slowly I was making up my mind to leave. To go back somehow to my mother.

No, not somehow! Now! Today! I felt a powerful energy rise up within me. I emptied the brown paper bags back on to my bed, and picked over the contents with new eyes. Selecting only the warmer clothing, I slid unwanted apparel under the covers while three women hovered over the corpse of Gran, taking no notice of me.

Down in the kitchen, I stuffed my tummy with as much food as I could hold, but, overwhelmed with excitement, my appetite was limited. Then I folded into a tea cloth some coarse bread, a lump of cheese, perhaps the ration for the lot of them, the jam-making sugar lumps, a slab of compressed dates and a few withered apples. On the back of a blue sugar bag I wrote to Mrs Jones.

> Dear Mrs Jones,
> My mother came and collected me by car to take me to Scotland. Sorry about Gran. Thank you.
> From,
> Marian.

The bold black carpenter pencil showed up well on the rather dark sugar bag. I set it up in a prominent position in front of the clock on the mantelpiece in the kitchen.

Then I left.

ELEVEN

Homing

It was approximately two weeks before Christmas. I remembered grating the carrots for the Christmas puddings on the second day I'd arrived at the Jones's. Well, I'd miss all that.

There were no road signs and, not by any means sure of the way, I racked my brains to try to remember the route I had come with the three little piggies. I went unnoticed through the village, past the little chapel and the vicar's cottage, and on the narrow open road.

The day was cold but clear, and already the frost had lifted. I felt elated at the thought of seeing Mummy again, and batted away a fleeting vision of black rage as one would swat a fly and think no more of it. Soon, confident at being out of earshot, I started singing, 'Oh show me the way to go home . . .', jazzing it up in time to my feet.

Walking for perhaps a couple of hours at a speedy pace I became aware of a great thirst; I realised that I'd had nothing at all to drink. I'd meant to take a can of cold tea, like the men, who snatched up their packets from the kitchen table. As I went up a steep hill the thirst became a passion. I bent down on the shaded side of the road and sucked at the grass still wet from the early morning frost.

Down in the valley I heard the sound of running water and I

sat beside a rivulet, cupped my hands into the sweet water, and ate with miserly reserve from my store.

Reluctantly I carried on, feeling stiff and cold. Then I heard in my head a voice from the past. 'Walk from the hip!' It was the cry of dear Miss Murk from the Orphanage. I tried it and instantly felt an ease of movement. Knowing that I had a mighty long walk ahead I blew her a grateful kiss.

'I wouldn't leave my little wooden house for you . . .' I sang, trying to cheer away the tiredness that was creeping over me. It was getting colder and I regretted the fact that I'd neglected to bring a blanket. Not a soul passed me all day and I saw no sign of a dwelling. I couldn't see past the scrub-covered banks on either side of the lane.

Now with the light fading almost imperceptibly, at perhaps only four o'clock in the afternoon, I had to find somewhere to sleep. Then I heard a dog bark in the distance and reasoning that he must have a home, hurried my pace. Less than half a mile along the lane, I saw cow dung on the road. I knew there must be a farm nearby, and sure enough the straggly growth above the verge changed to a neat hedge.

Not daring to open the gate, fearful of setting the dog barking, I climbed over it and crept stealthily along a tree-lined drive. Unexpectedly, I came across a turreted white-painted house beyond which I could see some neat brick outhouses. I made my way cautiously to these, keeping off the gravelled path, my feet treading the grass verge. I quietly searched in the dimming light through the low buildings for somewhere to sleep, but I felt only the cold bare bones of machinery.

Then I heard the soft snuffle of a horse. With some difficulty I found the barn that housed him and silently lifted the latch. Sure enough, a great beast stood there. Above was a gallery of stored hay. Gingerly skirting the horse, which regarded me with a suspicious eye, I climbed a fixed ladder. Then I made my way to the furthest corner, stretched out and ate as much as I dared, reminding myself sadly that the food must last a long time. That done, I buried myself in the hay and quickly fell asleep.

I started up instantly at hearing the sound of a cock crowing. As I did so, the horse was startled and began to move about, snorting and stamping. Fearful of discovery, my heart racing, I frantically felt around in the dark for the ladder. Inadvertently I loosed a bale of hay which fell to the ground near the horse. The terrified animal neighed like a trumpet. Panic rose within me as I remembered the long drop to the floor. Finally my hands felt the rough wood of the ladder and I shinned down, let myself out and ran along the edge of the path, passing the faint image of the house, and out over the gate. My legs were all atremble.

Now as I strode along the road I observed a faint lightening of the sky ahead of me. An old saying flashed into my head: 'The sun rises in the east and sets in the west.' In my mind's eye I could see the map of Britain, Wales was due west of London, so I must be sure to start into the sun each morning. I would have to consider that the sun moves around in the sky. This thought brought confusion. I must have looked a little crazy as I trotted along, two bags in one hand and the other pointing to the heavens, tracing in a muddled fashion the possible path of the sun. It occurred to me that sailors perhaps navigate the seas in this way.

As I went along, I nibbled at the cheese, tore at the bread and sucked a couple of sugar lumps. The stiffness that I'd suffered from at first melted away and I felt good, apart from a sudden thirst. I had on a good coat (a little big for me), two jumpers, two vests, ample bloomers, a skirt, grey wool socks and stout, comfortable shoes. In my bag I had another jumper, two pairs of bloomers, another skirt, two-and-a-half pairs of socks and my velour hat, all of which had been given to me, absolutely brand new, in the rest home. My wellingtons I had dumped in a ditch, as they were too heavy and cumbersome to walk in.

A light shone ahead. Someone wasn't strictly observing black-out conditions; then it flickered out. It would be really light soon; people would be moving about and would perhaps think it odd that I was walking alone so early. I turned the bend. Suddenly an engine burst into life beside me. I dived into the hedgerow and heard clanging and crashing that threatened to engulf me, then the engine and its noise receded and all became quiet.

Out of the hedge, I surveyed the scene and saw deposited on a rough table four battered milk churns. Carefully mounting the table, and seeing no one, I lifted the lid and scooped out the milk with my dirty hands. It was the sweetest, creamiest milk I'd ever tasted. Silently I replaced the lid, slid off the table and hurried along the verge, stopping only to wipe my hands on the crisp grass.

Although there was very little traffic on the road, I was constantly listening, and keeping an eye out for a possible hiding place, should I hear the approach of a vehicle. Later in the day, I went through a village, and was stared at with such intense curiosity that I worried about it. I fixed my eyes straight ahead and eventually passed the last house with immense relief.

On and on I went, up hills and down dales, until every muscle ached, and my legs seemed to go forward on their own. There seemed to be miles and miles of woodland which gave little prospect of shelter for the coming night, and I viewed the dark trees with some anxiety. Then I came across a clearing where I could see a little hut. Climbing some low railings, I quietly approached the entrance. On the door was a notice warning of the danger of fire. The door was unlocked and inside were fire brushes made from twigs lashed together, and a pile of sacks. I barred the door as best I could from the inside and crept under a fair bed of sacks and slept.

The next morning brought agony. I could barely move. Every part of me ached, but I ate a little and instantly revived and in no time I was stepping out upon the road. The slanting sun cheered me, although the wind was cold and the frost seemed to pinch at my bare knees. Very soon I felt at ease and I was back into the swing of my walk and singing at the top of my voice.

That day I passed an army camp on the fringes of the forest. Lorry after lorry trundled past me. Except for an occasional wave, the drivers took no notice of me, and I hurried on with the air of one with an early destination.

I came across a town which I believe now was Gloucester, but I cannot be sure. I do know that it was with some difficulty that I found the right road out of it as I had to ask the way to London. I did so by saying that 'my friend said it was that way, and I said it was this way'. It seemed that my fictitious friend and I were both wrong, for it was quite another.

Leaving behind the sharp hills, I walked through the country-side which was now rolling and barren, with little sign of life. My feet pounded along and I played little games, trying to move silently, like a cat; reciting aloud poetry, including the many nursery rhymes I could remember. Sometimes I'd get along in leaps and bounds by skipping and dancing, but I found a steady stride less tiring.

That night was spent in the open, in a haystack. I managed to climb up, and with some strenuous heaving and tugging, burrowed into the soggy mass. I soon became aware that I was sharing my nest with an army of small rodents and all sorts of creepy-crawlies, so I covered my head completely with my spare jumper. Only the coarse spiky hay sticking into me bothered me. Eventually I settled down, and nursing my raw fingers sank into sweet oblivion.

It was light when I emerged. The chilly damp had left my limbs rigid. I noticed, as I delved painfully into one of the bags for the last of the cheese, that two of my fingers had festered. The bread, apples and sugar gone, only some dates were left.

Somehow I had to replenish my stocks.

The sky was overcast, the night had been without frost and I soon became warmed by the exercise of my swinging legs. The ominous blackness of the clouds threatened rain and I was going through territory that promised no shelter. As usual in the face of adversity, I started to sing. This time I searched my memory for the old choruses that we used to sing in the Orphanage. One for every letter of the alphabet:

'Absolutely tender, absolutely true, understanding all things, understanding you . . .'

'Because my Saviour, He loves me, He loves me, He loves me. My heart goes singing all the day . . .'

'Can you hear the voice of Jesus, calling, calling you? Can you . . .'

'Draw your swords, use your swords, for the battle is the Lord's. Trust in his . . .'

right through to 'Zacarrus was a little man, and a very little man was he . . .' Thus I amused myself, for I loved these extravagant choruses. They had helped to mould my ideas of love and feed my sense of drama. As I rolled the words carefully around my tongue, I savoured the expression of passion and the conjured images, yet I felt oddly detached.

Although I was, of course, quite damned, I was beginning to doubt the very existence of God. I'd read parts of the Bible that made God sound every bit as bad as the Devil. Now I looked up at the black clouds a little fearfully. If God really existed, per-haps He'd strike me dead. Then I dared Him to!

Mrs Jones had been surprised that I would sit so absorbed for so long reading her family Bible, but it was still my favourite book. What would people think, I wondered, if I picked out the passages where God's wrath was fearsome, as He amused Himself by destroying wicked men, their wives and, of course, their little children who'd had nothing to do with their old dads' iniquity! The stoning of people was fully approved of by Him. 'Bloody God,' I shouted to the thunderous clouds.

This great journey exercised more than my wits and my feet. It was my first great unfettered 'Think'. I thought on the business of free will. My father had killed himself, and deprived us of a chance of being a family. Somebody else's free will had blasted away a home and love from one of 'My poor little ones'. What of some of the children from the Orphanage, who would never be able to work things out for themselves?

Now it occurred to me that this free will idea couldn't possibly be a personal thing, and therefore 'free will' didn't really exist. My thoughts wandered into complicated paths in a rather muddled way, but somehow these meanderings lessened my fears of divine retribution.

I loved Jesus and I was filled with regret and a sort of guilt mixed with defiance. I was terribly sorry that I had led a life of shame, but I wouldn't beg forgiveness, not me! Yet I bitterly wished I could be humble, be good. Then I shrugged the thoughts away. Regrets were no use. They didn't change things. It was evident that I would have to shelve these ideas for the more practical task of finding shelter for the coming downpour.

So my journey went. Somehow my feet always pointed in the right direction. I obtained food in a number of ways. Once, not trusting adults, I spoke to a couple of small children saying that I'd run away from 'bad' people and needed food. I challenged their ability to keep a secret. I waited with some anxiety as they scurried off, but they returned bringing me a fine feast. I ate Brussels sprouts and raw turnips caked with hard mud, and I dug into a frozen mountain of swedes. I became wise about milk churns and waited for them. Once I took a billy-can and thick sandwiches and sweet hot tea that had been left on one of the typical rough tables outside a farm.

My muscles became hard and I felt strong. My face and hands and the backs of my knees were chapped and sore, so I no longer tried to wipe them clean. The handles of the carrier bags had long since given out and I now had them tied with string I'd found on the road.

Then I had a bad day.

The previous night had been bitterly cold and for a long time I could find no shelter, so I had carried on walking on the slippery road in the moonlight. Finally I turned into a narrow lane and bedded down in a smelly outhouse attached to a little cottage. In the morning I was woken by an old man shuffling about. I watched him from under a pile of carpeting and rubbish. After a while he sat on an elsan lavatory, gurgling and spluttering as he painfully emptied the contents of his bowels, all the time groaning and cursing and emitting a frightful pong!

As soon as I dared I was back on the road, but I had no food and felt a great weariness. Sometimes, that day, it seemed as though I almost floated along. I didn't even fling myself into a ditch at the sound of a car or lorry, I just kept on. As darkness approached I observed a policeman coming towards me on a bicycle. As he passed, I looked the other way. I glanced behind me at this retreating figure and saw him turn. He did not see me dart behind a hedge and lie flat on the ground. I lay there listening to his bicycle weaving backwards and forwards until he eventually gave up.

I didn't hear the car coming up behind me, but I stopped in my tracks when it drew alongside. The policeman (he had no hat on, but I knew that he was a policeman) spoke to me.

'Run away, have we?'

I nodded.

'Going far, then?'

I nodded again.

'Want a lift, then?'

Another nod and I climbed into the car and promptly fell asleep.

Next thing I knew, I was sitting on a chair and a woman was holding my hand while the policeman took off my shoes. I couldn't keep my eyes open but I listened to them talking about me.

'She's come a long way, unless I'm mistaken, look at these!'

Then my hands were manipulated. 'My goodness! Look at these hands. For crying out loud!'

'Put her in a hot bath, love. I warrant that'd make her feel a lot better.'

The warmth of the house was stifling and I struggled to keep awake. I became aware that the wife was looking through the pockets of my coat.

'Nothing here. What's your name, dear?' she said.

'Maisie. Maisie Stock.'

'Where are you from?'

'I . . . I can't remember!' That's it! I've lost my memory!

'We're not going to get much out of her tonight. Best do that bath, find her something to eat and put her to bed.' The dear policeman couldn't have put it better.

The policeman's wife bathed me in scalding water with much sympathetic oh-dearing, then smothered me in Germolene. I was put in one of her flannel nighties and carried downstairs by her husband. In the kitchen I was fed, while my fingers were bandaged. Declining the offer of a lift up the stairs, I followed his wife who showed me the way to a tiny room. I tumbled into the bed and, promising myself that I'd be on the road before they awoke, fell asleep.

The sun was as high as it could get on that winter's day when I eventually opened my eyes. My clothes were nowhere to be seen. I looked into a mirror on the dressing table. My face was shiny and cherry red! I went down the stairs and saw, to my dismay, that my clothes had been washed with the exception of my coat, which the wife was sponging at the sink.

'Feeling better?'

'Yes, thank you.'

She busied herself with making my breakfast. She chatted a bit, but asked no questions then. I offered no comments and kept my eyes on my food. The day was spent lying about and listening to the wireless. This was my first experience with a wireless and I became determined that I'd have one in my palace. The machine totally fascinated me. As I twiddled the knobs I discovered, to my amazement, that people really did speak different languages. The music and songs thrilled me and, for the first time, I listened to the news.

The policeman and his wife left me pretty much to myself. That evening they tried to question me, but 'I can't remember!' was all they could get out of me.

Later that evening I listened to the wireless, I pricked up my ears, for I heard them discussing me in the kitchen. The man said that they'd hang on to me for a couple of days and that I was no trouble. No one had reported me missing, but they'd trace me all right.

By the evening all my clothes were neatly deposited upon a chair in the room I slept in. I promptly made up my mind to leave at the crack of dawn if the weather was good, for now it was raining. But the next morning it was still raining, so I passed another day, somewhat anxiously, resting with the wireless.

Early the next day I was charging towards the faintest haze of light far on the horizon. I had stuffed my clothes in a pillowcase, the white linen hidden by pushing the whole thing into my spare navy jumper and tying the arms to make a handle. Also

I had helped myself to a little of everything from their larder, except the meat. I didn't care for meat.

Straining my ears for the sound of a car, I more than once got soaked by jumping into ditches.

For days I carried on, spending many nights in good places, and eventually found myself in Epping Forest, which seemed full of soldiers.

I felt good! I felt strong! I could have walked to the end of the world! Now I was on the very edge of London. I found myself laughing. I could do anything.

I told a soldier that I'd lost my fare, and was given enough money to buy a ticket on the underground for the last bit of the journey. I got on the train at Epping and smiled at those who puckered their noses and looked me up and down. I got off at Queensway station.

Then, with the top of my head touching the sky, I swung with long triumphant strides, in a mood of unspeakable excitement, to Mummy and home.

TWELVE

George

As I mounted the stairs I felt a pain of longing to see Mummy again. Then, hearing the sounds of raucous laughter coming from above, my step faltered. Must be George. 'Compassionate leave.' The words came back to me. Still it would have to be faced. With the explosive joy I had felt turned to hesitancy, I burst into the flat.

Mummy gave me a startled look of disbelief.

Two American soldiers were sitting at her feet, another sprawled across the floor. The four of them just stared at me and said nothing. Mummy, speechless, pointed in the direction of the kitchen.

For a moment I stood there surveying the scene. The room was hot and smoky, littered with the signs of an earlier feast. Then Mummy's eyes flashed angrily, and another imperious gesture sent me scuttling to the kitchen. She scurried after me and closed the door.

'What is the meaning of this?' she cried in a furious whisper. 'Where have you come from? Christ Almighty! Do you know what you look like?'

The words stung. My exultation was crushed. I felt my face burn, but Mummy had left, shutting the kitchen door behind her.

A moment later, I heard her sing out: 'Boys, give us a

moment. I'll have to see to this wench. Turn the wireless on. I'll be ready soon.'

I jumped as Mummy unexpectedly returned. Then I slowly walked round the kitchen table, dusting the tops of the chairs as I did so, before coming to a halt. I faced her with some trepidation.

'For God's sake, don't look at me like that. You gave me quite a shock! You look odd, all arms and legs.' She was taking coppers out of her purse. 'Have a bath and go to bed. I'm going out. They came to take me out.'

Noticing that she was all dressed up, I smiled.

'Go on, Mummy. It's all right.'

'We'll talk about everything in the morning.'

Alone, I grabbed at the nearest food and walked around the flat nursing a longed-for cup of tea. I found the wireless Mummy spoke of and quickly tuned to a jazz programme, turning up the volume full blast before wandering into what had been my room.

Nothing of mine was left there. Someone else had taken possession of the room. Men's clothes were strewn around a kit-bag on the floor. Rushing to Mummy's room, I found no evidence of such an intrusion, but in Anthony's I saw the same signs of occupation, and the bathroom, too, was littered with their things.

Too tired to think about it now, I had a leisurely bath, turned off the wireless, slipped into one of Mummy's silky crêpe dresses and slid into her bed.

The days that followed were mostly happy. Mummy got over her initial shock at seeing me. She never asked what had happened to me for the last three months and I didn't volunteer any information. She just seemed to accept the fact that I was there.

The soldiers were on leave and seemed happy to have Mummy's company. I proudly observed her remarkable ability to discuss authoritatively many subjects, some very new to me. They delighted in her mischievous sense of humour and they were themselves great fun, calling me 'Honeybunch'. I was immediately included in daytime activities.

In the evenings, I was left to my own devices, which included putting everything in order, and they'd congratulate Mummy for having brought me up so well. The remark sent Mummy and me into hysterical giggles. This perplexed the Americans who wished to be let in on our secret.

My arrival home was just two days before the new year. The soldiers celebrated by buying me new clothes, filling our larder with canned food and showering us with many gifts. Just a few days later, we said farewell.

Mummy was immensely relieved at their departure, for she had begun to feel unwell. They had exhausted her. Immediately after they left, she threw off her clothes and took to her bed, where she stayed while I pursued my own solitary life.

Now and then Mummy would get up for a few days and somehow acquire some money. I made it plain that I was disinclined to steal. As the bounty left by the soldiers dissipated, we needed a minimum of food. Mummy didn't care about food and wanted to spend our very limited funds on cigarettes, which brought bitter irrational arguments between us, threatening possible violence. In the end, driven by hunger and the need to pacify Mummy's special need, I succumbed. At first I lifted just this and that, but eventually stealing once more became second nature to me and I found it easier than ever.

By now I had become aware of the differences in people's lifestyles, the uneven distribution of available goods, and I had begun to question things. But I never questioned the way we lived. I knew the cause of our aberrated existence was Mummy's mental illness. If she was to escape being locked up in an horrendous institution – a situation she feared most dreadfully – she would have to be protected and her condition hidden. There was no place in accepted society for the likes of us, and no help available.

I acquired a large, beautifully sprung, old pram and took to helping myself to coal from the railways and picking up discarded vegetables after the street markets had closed. I walked for miles with my eyes glued to the pavements in search of the odd coin.

Twilight and a winter fog once availed me of a much-needed opportunity. In the otherwise deserted streets, I happened to spot a man by the open back doors of his van. He was peering at a piece of paper and then towards the elegant houses on the other side of the street. He marched off with a box, and I swiftly and neatly deposited many cartons of groceries into the old pram and silently disappeared into the fog. The pillage, which included cigarettes, caused Mummy to bounce out of her bed and we ate and giggled as we imagined the poor fellow in the act of discovering his loss.

One day when scavenging for coal, I found an abandoned bicycle on top of a heap of rubbish in the railway yard. I hauled it on to the ground and, by sheer perseverance over many days, mastered the ramshackle thing. Soon I was picking up bicycles, bicycles with brakes, and joy-riding all over London. Preferring ladies', I also learned to hare about on men's bicycles by standing and leaning from side to side.

Somewhere in Hammersmith I found myself walking my bike through a street market. A man with a colourful patter was extolling the virtue of second-hand bicycles. He eyed my rather smart racer with envy, offering thirty shillings for it. In no time, I had his money and a promise that he would buy others if my friends would wish me to act on their behalf. This became a new source of income. It was easy at the time and I gave little thought to those I robbed.

The 'Fagan of the Bikes' became a friend. He was cheery and

extremely funny. Even while he placed orders for the kind of bicycle he preferred, he begged me to give up the practice. But Mummy was happy with the money, never asking me how I obtained the goodies I brought home. Indeed she'd hold out her hands delightedly to catch the cigarettes and call me 'my angel'.

This income came to an end. I arrived one day in the market just in time to see my friend being helped into a black sedan by uniformed policemen. An excited array of stallholders was gathered around his wares. Fearing my familiarity would encourage a finger pointed in my direction, I streaked away, sure that Scotland Yard was on my tail.

Later I tried to sell stolen bikes to shops, but found that a receipt was required. Sensing an air of deep suspicion had been aroused, I retreated hastily from what was to be my last shop, and vowed never to steal another bicycle.

Occasionally I'd spend happy, animated days with Mummy, when we'd sit together listening to the wireless, or chat, each with our own occupation. She would perhaps write to George, while I'd make passable garments for myself from her discarded clothing. Mummy would praise my stitching and I'd show off my trick of threading a fine needle with my eyes closed. At these times she was so charming and adorable, and seemed so clever and wise, that I'd catch my breath, knowing that she was so sadly afflicted.

Never again did I suffer a battering.

I now knew the warning signs of a potential eruption of violence. Lifting my bed-roll, I would disappear until I judged my mother's fears had burned themselves out. She now thought that she was being spied upon, that outer space intelligences were interfering with her thoughts and actions. She would shout curses at them or beg that they leave her alone. Then she would snap out of it, and be loving and amusing, even industrious. But I was always on my guard, always alert to her mood.

It was at this time that she gave a graphic account of how we children had been snatched away from her. My father's suicide had left her distraught and penniless, living in a single room in a filthy house, one of a row in a no-man's-land near the gasworks. She had four tiny children, all hungry. Crushed by grief and the knowledge of how far she'd come down in the world, she could do nothing but rock with the little ones in her arms.

'Hours later,' she told me, 'there was a shuffling at the door. Then it was quiet. Again something moved outside, and I heard a door close somewhere in the house. I got in a rage. I sprang to the door and was ready to strike. But I saw that little gifts of food, from those who had nothing, were placed on the floor. Two apples, a part of a loaf of bread and a half wrapped piece of sausage meat.'

She snatched up the food, took out the back of the drawers from a chest (she had already burned the boards from under the bed) and lit a fire on which to cook a meagre supper.

Neighbours could not help her when she was evicted for being unable to pay the rent. She had been to the National Assistance Board, the Church Army, the Distressed Gentlewomen . . . and all she had was one shilling.

'I have no money,' she said quietly to the menacing landlord.

'Now, Miss High and Mighty, come, come. You've still got your looks.' The odious man leaned right over her. 'We could come to some arrangement.'

She screamed at him, calling him scum.

He threw her out – into the street, with her barefoot children and a baby in her arms. Faces popped out of doors as she cursed the landlord, before striding away, head in the air. Later, she went back, for blankets and her few possessions.

'The next night found us on Paddington Station,' she told me. 'I was exhausted. My arms seemed to be pulled from me. I laid you all on a seat. The roar of the steam trains and the incessant clanging and shunting of the trolleys were like the rage in my head.'

It was from this bench at Paddington Station that her children were removed from her, literally wrenched from her arms. Millicent and Dorothy, aged six and five respectively, were placed in Spurgeon's Orphanage in Stockwell, London. Anthony, three, went somewhere in Brixton and later to Spurgeon's. And Marian? Just six months old I entered Lady Montague Home, an orphanage for infants in Brixton, London.

'They took my babies,' my mother groaned, 'and put me into the pit of Hell. And then they said I was mad and put me in a loony bin. I couldn't come to that awful place, that Orphanage. I loved you all so. I couldn't bear it. I had to get on with my life.'

As she bitterly revisited those dark days, sometimes oblivious of my presence, her anger would grow and she'd beg and plead for her babies.

I discovered the British Museum. I stood in awe in front of the colossal legacy of a previous civilisation, was fascinated by the mummies, and selected many more objects to include in the palace of my dreams. I would dream of a better life, bitterly regretting my own circumstances in which I seemed so trapped. Then I'd cheerfully throw out such thoughts and resign myself, thinking of the game of 'One day . . . in my palace . . .' But I knew that I was being silly, it was no use dwelling on fantasy. I had to grow up a bit. Perhaps when George came back from the Far East? I now looked forward to the practical possibilities of his presence. Perhaps he'd know what to do.

The months passed, my thirteenth birthday came and went with no marking of the event. A hint of summer had us out once more on the Bayswater Road, making for the countryside. We arrived, by the haphazard direction of our transport, at Spoon-bed Farm, where we spent a pleasant season, marred only by the manner of our leaving.

We were thrown off the farm with the aid of the police. Mummy had made the life of the farmer's wife a misery by not paying for anything and proffering violence when insistent, irritating slips of paper, itemising goods received, were pinned upon our tent.

The exasperated police didn't know whom to believe. Mummy's educated manners and ladylike display of effrontery at the unreasonable accusations of the farmer's wife were more coherent than the protests of the poor hard-working lady who somehow was made to seem so inferior.

On the train home, which was paid for by the police, we laughed and made merry. Somehow Mummy had convinced the police that it was she who had been robbed. I was sad about it, and vowed I'd go back one day and make it up to the farmer's wife who'd been kind to us.

In London the air raids seemed to have halted. Even in the parks the army was packing up the great guns and making more space available to the public. Now we had the Doodlebugs. These low-flying, rocket-propelled bombs were fearsome things. The sound of one passing overhead would fill me with dread, for now I was suddenly afraid. Listening, I'd wait for the motor to cut out and the subsequent almighty exploding thump, and then carry on with immense relief.

In the late autumn, George came home on compassionate leave.

Mummy rose early. She looked thin and pale when I brought her a cup of tea. A fog of cigarette smoke greeted me. George's letters were strewn over the bed and her clothes were flung about the room. I knew she hadn't slept all night.

'No nonsense, my girl,' she said unreasonably.

'Don't worry, Mummy. Everything will be fine.'

With a feeling of apprehension, I left her and busied myself by putting the finishing touches to the rest of the flat.

Over an hour passed. She is too quiet, I thought anxiously. I peeped round her door. She was lying on top of her bed, softly snoring. I crept in. As I gently covered her, and silently inched open the window, I wondered what time George would arrive, and whether Mummy would behave herself, and what he'd think of me.

Mummy slept for hours. It was four o'clock when I brought her tea again.

'Christ!' she exploded. 'Are you mad? You think I want him to see me like this?'

'It's all right Mummy.' I was already swiftly tidying her room. 'I've run your bath. Come on, drink your tea.'

'Dear God! I've nothing to wear,' she said embracing the great heaps of clothing with a flourish of her hand.

'I'll chose your outfit. You'll look stunning now you've had a sleep. Go on, get in your bath now.'

Much to my relief she went like a lamb.

'I'm supposed to be *your* damn mother,' she called out on her way to the bathroom.

An hour later Mummy did indeed look stunning. I'd chosen and pressed a slim black costume and a white blouse with a low neckline. Her black high-heeled court shoes were put out and I'd draped her fox fur, handbag, underwear and corset upon the bed in the now immaculate room.

'You're an absolute treasure, darling,' Mummy said delightfully over tea and toast in the kitchen. 'I needed that sleep.'

George arrived with perfect timing.

We heard his slow tread up the stairs. Mummy stood in the hall facing the entrance to the flat, patting herself nervously. I shot into the kitchen and peeped through a crack in the almost-closed door.

I liked him instantly.

He dropped his duffle bag and other parcels just inside the door, swept off his Air Force cap, and eagerly stepped towards Mummy.

'Leanora. I'm here, at last,' he said softly.

(That, of course, was her name. Strangely, I'd never heard anyone say it before.)

Mummy flung herself at him. 'Oh Georgie, I've had such a hard time.'

Much to my surprise, he didn't kiss her. He seemed to hold her awkwardly.

'There, there. It's all right, old girl. I'll take care of you now.'

Mummy turned and called to me.

'Where are you, my little scamp? Come and kiss your Daddy.'

I came out of my hiding-place and looked at Mummy, but she avoided my gaze. I dutifully stretched up on my toes and kissed George's cheek. He gave me a lovely smile.

'My, you're a pretty girl,' he said sweetly.

He looked and behaved like an absolute gentleman. His quiet attention to Mummy caused her to glow prettily and she was very happy. He was exceedingly kind to me.

George brought money with him. We shopped for groceries and I kept the flat spotless, so that our lives took on an unaccustomed normality. In a while he left us, to return shortly in his demob suit to pursue a new career.

I was never to go hungry again. But the good life did not continue.

Mummy's affability quickly degenerated. George had got himself a job as a porter in a very swish block of flats. One evening, shortly after he left for work, she suddenly sprang from her room where she had been resting.

'He's gone again, has he?'

'Yes, Mummy. He didn't want to disturb you.'

'I bet he didn't,' she hissed. 'He's got a floozie.' She was throwing his pyjamas across the room and dressing herself with great speed.

'Please, Mummy, don't,' I said helplessly.

Her eyes were wild as she violently pushed past me.

'You mind your own business,' she said savagely.

I surprised myself worrying about George. I thought miserably: She'll shatter everything, but of course I knew she would. She can't help herself. He'll go.

Alone, to blot out my mind, I sang mournfully, 'Oh, for the wings, for the wings of a dove . . .', and then cheerfully, 'Where the bee sucks, there suck I. In a cowslip's bell I lie.'

George didn't go.

Mummy lost his job for him by creating dreadful scenes. He immediately got another position and the same thing happened. Mummy then made his life a living hell, accusing him of unfaithfulness and all sorts of imagined evils. Soon he took on a haunted, haggard appearance. She seemed to delight in tormenting him. One day she threw all his clothes into the fireplace and set light to them.

The atmosphere at home became unbearable. More than once the new tenants downstairs, hearing the ranting and screams of abuse coming from our flat, called the police. George obeyed her every demand issued in a cruelly despising manner. Eventually, I begged him to leave her.

It was while escaping this misery that I was once more caught shoplifting.

My first instinct when approached was to run, but this was made impossible by the fact that a rather large lady was holding my arm in a gentle yet vice-like grip. I felt the blood drain from my face as I was marched almost casually to the manager's office. The manager was a very righteous man with a very large head, which he thrust inches from my face, frightening me. I refused to give my name. I didn't want George to know me as a thief. Whereupon I was left with the large lady who gave me kindly smiles. We waited silently for the police to arrive. I was offered a sandwich, but I refused; my mouth was dry. Two policewomen duly arrived and I was taken to the police station, deposited in a cell, and told 'not to worry'.

The cell was about eight feet long by four feet wide and tiled like a public lavatory. After some hours I was taken to an office where my fingers were rolled on to a black inking pad while a nice policeman chatted out of me the secret of my identity. Mummy arrived, advised the police of my criminal nature, and in the same breath begged that she be allowed to take her poor baby home. It seemed that she convinced the police that I was indeed a hardened thief. She eventually left the station in a rage of grief and I heard her threatening all sorts of violence.

I found myself once more in the same remand centre that I'd been in so long ago. No one seemed to remember me and I saw no familiar faces. I thought of nothing but escaping and, with this in mind, kept a very low profile of complete obedience, until one day, just before lunch, I saw a possibility.

Always extremely agile, I somehow climbed a low building and leapt up on to a high wall which surrounded the place. Here there was some kind of obstruction, perhaps broken glass, which ripped at my flesh. But it was the sheer drop on the other side that caused my insides to shrink. Already hearing cries behind me, my hesitation ceased and I dropped down, surprisingly unhurt, and raced away on foot until I stole an overlarge bicycle and tore along the streets to my familiar old hidy-hole.

It is difficult to express the misery I felt when the impact of my position dawned upon me. I couldn't go home. That was where *they* would look for me. I could no longer bear the prospect of Mummy. Renewing my life at home would bring no joy. I thought of asking George to help me, but shelved that idea. He was such a good man and I was too ashamed. Having cut myself off from decent society by my own actions, I felt the enormity of my isolation. I was covered from the waist down in caked blood, and I rolled into a ball. There I stayed, in a damp hole in the ground feeling mighty sorry for myself until darkness fell.

Not knowing what else I could do, I painfully made my way home.

The hue and cry after me did not materialise. Mummy bathed my wounds tenderly and took care of me sweetly until I healed. George took a temporary job away from home, helping to run a small hotel for an Air Force friend. We were not short of money, but without him around Mummy was subdued. She expressed fears that she had lost him. She said that she hadn't been able to help herself in the way she had treated him.

Inevitably, Mummy took to her bed and I roamed the streets. Inevitably, I was nabbed again.

This time I was taken to more secure custody. They seemed to know all about me and I attended a Juvenile Court, where the magistrate called for a psychiatric report. When I heard these words, I understood them to suspect that I was perhaps mad. I visualised the possibility of myself being locked into Mummy's nightmare.

It turned out to be not as bad as I feared. It was decided that I was malnourished and I was given a special diet. A probation officer chatted with me daily.

Her friendliness amazed me, for she seemed even to like me. The psychiatrist gave me all sorts of puzzles and pictures of the utmost simplicity to put in order and asked me innumerable questions. A rather severe lady, I thought, and quite odd.

She asked me if I wished to go to school and study for a career. I told her that I hated that idea and was anxious to take my punishment. I would be fourteen in six months' time when I could earn my own living. The psychiatrist smiled and said that I was not going to be punished, but, together with the probation officer, she really had to work out my future. She also said that I had great possibilities and that it would be a pity to waste such potential for a useful life. She added that she didn't think that I was a really bad girl.

So I waited, with no thoughts of escape, for what might be in store for me. It seemed that I must go to an approved school. Although the psychiatrist had said that I would not benefit from a further stay in an institution, they were at a loss as to what to do with me. With desperate feelings of dejected resignation, I made up my mind to make the best of the situation.

It was while leaning against the wall in the common room, and feeling apprehensive and sad, that I saw the probation officer bounding towards me. Her face was full of smiles and she grasped my hands as she told me that she'd found me somewhere very special to go. So it was, in a few days, that I arrived, duly kitted out, at the house of Miss Cole.

THIRTEEN

My Champion

Miss Cole had snow-white hair tied behind her head in a large untidy bun, and she was quite fat. She looked shyly at the probation officer and then spoke to me.

'Well, Marian, the Lord has brought you to me!' She took my hand. 'Come, I always show the garden first. One is nearer to God in the garden, don't you think?'

It was a lovely garden. Quite the prettiest I had ever seen. A formal terraced lawn swept away from the house, bordered on either side by sweet-smelling low lavender hedges holding in check riotous coloured blooms. The garden fell away to a delightful wild wooded dell, blackberry bushes and a trickle of a stream.

While we walked Miss Cole haltingly explained that she took in girls of exceptional ability, who were able to take advantage of an education under the protection of her house. She had been, many years ago, the headmistress of a girls' school, and felt that she could still help in this way. She had other girls; they had been casualties of the war or had inappropriate homes. It seemed that I came under the latter category.

Miss Cole lifted a stone and showed me a newt. Soon we were both kneeling, examining insects and spiders like a couple of enthusiastic children, and making friends. We heard the chiming of a bell in the distance.

'Oh dear! How time goes!' she cried.

Together we hurried back and strode across the lawn, where she stopped breathlessly for a moment, anxiously regarding me.

'I must tell you, Marian, I think we'll get along. I know you've had a very difficult time, but here you start with a clean slate.' With that she closed her eyes and prayed. 'Dear Lord Jesus, help this Thy child to know Thy ways. Protect her from all evil, and show her Thy path. Amen!'

To my surprise, the probation officer, who had brought me here, had waited all this time just inside the gate. Miss Cole led me into the house, and deposited me on a chair while she went out again to chat to the probation officer. The two of them returned and Miss Cole left me alone with the probation officer.

'Now, Marian, you passed with flying colours!' I looked at her quizzically. 'Your walk in the garden! That was an interview!' She smiled, then her face clouded. 'Now, my dear, this really is your last chance. I have great faith in you. Don't let me down, will you?'

'No, I won't, and thank you for everything,' I said earnestly.

'Bye then, take care.' And she was gone.

I was shown over the rambling Georgian country house that had perhaps once stood on its own. A long glasshouse leaned to a sidewall and contained antiquated heating devices that had rusted away. Miss Cole couldn't resist a hurried fussing over a couple of potted plants, wiping her hands carelessly on her hips as she chatted a little awkwardly.

'The other girls are older than you. They go to the grammar school. They're all doing very well. You know, we live very simply. Oh, I'll tell the girls that you are staying because your mother is sick, all right? It's quite true, isn't it?'

Inside was a large untidy kitchen, an airy sitting-room with a pair of french windows opening out to the garden, and a dark panelled library. Upstairs were innumerable bedrooms, one of which I was to share with two other girls.

Then she left me to wander about the house at will.

The girls arrived later in the afternoon. I watched them from an upstairs room as they came dashing through the gate in a noisy confident rush. As they entered, they seemed to fill the whole house, and the gentle quiet atmosphere was shattered. I couldn't bear the prospect of meeting them. Miss Cole called out to me, but I thrust my head out of the window so I could not hear her.

'Do you like my garden then?' Miss Cole was standing next to me. 'I must confess, I do feel so guilty sometimes. I do spend so much time out there!'

'Well, it's really lovely, Miss Cole,' I said.

'Oh, I'm so glad you like it!' she exclaimed emphatically as she squeezed my arm.

I followed her down the stairs and was introduced to the girls. They acknowledged me with brief polite smiles, then quickly assumed an attitude of indifference to my presence. I was greatly relieved and surprised that it had been so easy.

After tea, we had a reading from the Bible, a prayer and a hymn. I couldn't lift up my voice with the other girls. For some time now, I'd ceased singing and remained silent despite encouraging gestures from Miss Cole. I could not, in any case, sing the praises of One who so utterly condemned me.

When the prayers were over, the girls settled down to do their homework. Partly in an effort to be friendly, and also out of curiosity, I asked one of the girls if I could look at her books. She allowed me to glance over a well-thumbed arithmetic primer. It was beyond my comprehension. These clever girls would perhaps think me stupid, I thought with some dismay. Feeling ill at ease, I wandered away and sought the company of Miss Cole.

She was in the kitchen, about to wash the dishes. Picking up a tea towel, I helped while we talked of my future. It seemed that Miss Cole was to instruct me, until perhaps I too could attend the grammar school. Then the conversation came around to religion. Did I know the power of the Lord? Did I know Paul, who as Saul had murdered Christians, but after seeing the Light, was saved by the Power Divine? With religious fervour mounting within her, she suddenly pulled me to my knees on the kitchen floor and lifted up her arms in supplication.

'Oh, my child! Oh dear lost Child, repeat these words with me. "I believe. Help Thou mine unbelief!" Oh dear Lord Jesus hear Thy child!' Miss Cole nudged me into further passionate pleas. 'I believe. Help Thou mine unbelief!'

At first, as I observed Miss Cole's ridiculous wobbling jowls and avoided her floundering arms, I was almost overcome with a fit of the giggles. But then as she repeated the phrase over and over again, I was struck with her sincere passion, and I joined in the cry, bitterly wishing that indeed I might believe and find salvation. Yet, even then, in my heart of hearts, I knew that I could never believe in anything without practical evidence.

Later, on these occasions we would discuss an array of subjects on equal terms with the utmost seriousness. She seemed surprised and sometimes delighted when I confided my perhaps odd reasonings. There was something sweetly childish about her that I found endearing. Her greatest sadness was my difficulty in embracing the concepts of Christianity. Because of this, she could not, she felt, create a permanent change in me.

The weeks that followed were peaceful. Miss Cole's life was busy and constantly interrupted by callers, so that she made few attempts at giving me lessons. In fact she seemed scatty at times, and was content to find me an avid reader. Occasionally, I was given history or geography books to read, and we would have enjoyable question-and-answer sessions. We spent a lot of time in her garden, and I felt that she was developing a special regard for me as I shared her delight in nature.

Miss Cole went to innumerable 'meetings', always dragging

me along with her. I rather suspected that she had confided in her friends about my dismal fall from grace. They regarded me with curiosity and would tell me of erstwhile criminals who had undergone a complete change after they had allowed Jesus into their hearts. I was to have frequent reminders, one way or another, of my past sins. Certainly I wished to be 'good', but I didn't wish to lose my identity, or become like any of these people.

In desperation, Miss Cole took me to see Billy Graham the evangelist. I listened as he stormed about the vileness of the people present, and how Christ had died that terrible death on the cross for our sins. My mind wandered into thinking of the many people who had been crucified in this manner, as it had been a typical form of execution in those days. He talked of God's compassion for us and, in the same breath, violently decried the wicked world and yelled out impending doom. As his voice rose and his arms thrashed about him, the man struck a vague fear in me. I thought only of the insane rages of my mother and the newsreel rantings of Adolf Hitler. My instincts shied away from him and clinched my wariness to let go of the essence of me, which might be my soul.

Five months passed and I was nearly fourteen years of age. I became aware that I had been placed in the care of the Croydon Education Authority, since my mother had been declared an 'unfit' person. Miss Cole accepted my aversion to the grammar school and was now concerned that I should find suitable employment. She suggested some kind of library post and the two of us duly went to the Croydon office for their approval.

We were shown into a large bare-boarded room with rickety chairs, a kitchen-like table and dirty windows. It seemed that we had arrived just as the staff took their lunch break, so we, too, briefly slipped out for refreshments.

'You have wasted ten minutes of my precious time!' the ponderous man shouted as he tapped his watch.

I disliked him instantly. His insensitive, overbearing manner spelled out all I feared in puffed-up authority. He sat on the edge of the table holding a buff-coloured folder.

'Right nice little lady, aren't you?' he sneered sarcastically as he thumbed through the documents.

'Miss Hughes is a highly intelligent young woman.' Miss Cole had coloured deeply and her voice was crisp. 'She is quite capable of adapting herself, with a little training, to the needs of a library. Perhaps . . .'

The awful man threw back his head and thrust the file at Miss Cole. 'A library?' he scoffed. 'She's had no schooling at all! You want to tell me that she's even literate?'

'Have you read the file?' Miss Cole asked quietly.

'You think I've nothing better to do than go through this lot?' He tossed the file on to the table. Its contents spewed on to the floor. I leapt to gather up the papers, but was rudely pushed away. 'Don't you dare touch those!'

'I was merely picking it up for you!' I said as I darted back.

'Merely. Merely! Don't you come that high-falutin manner with me, Miss! I've read enough of what you've been up to and the kind of home you come from!'

He stepped towards me. 'Listen, Miss, you may have hoodwinked this old lady, but not me, Miss! Not me!'

I fought an overwhelming desire to spit in his face.

Miss Cole took my hand. 'We're wasting our time here. Come!'

He shouted after us. 'You come back here! I can still have you put away!' I hesitated, but Miss Cole tugged at me and we were out of the room in an instant.

Dear, dear Miss Cole, I thought, as we marched determinedly out of the building. Over seventy, yet Miss Cole had been my champion! What might have happened to me had I not had her at my side.

Outside in the street, Miss Cole took both my hands. 'Don't mind him, that man is of the Devil!' I hugged her and she returned my affection, pushing away a tear. We raced off hand in hand.

Miss Cole wished me to have a respectable occupation, of which I, or rather she, should not be ashamed. With some difficulty she eventually found me a post as a junior clerk in a solicitor's office in Lincoln's Inn Fields.

The following Monday morning I duly arrived, rather unfortunately attired in a discarded school uniform. I was dressed in a gymslip, a crisp white slightly darned blouse, white ankle socks and well-polished black shoes, with my satchel containing my sandwiches slung on my back. Thus I presented myself at the austere doors of Messrs. Marks & Clerks.

I was immediately taken under the scraggy wing of Miss Weller, a formidable lady who eyed me with obvious distaste.

'Your duties are to clean the offices, causing no inconvenience or noise. You will run messages and fetch and carry. I'll expect you to make tea, and perhaps you will progress to the filing room. I have been here for thirty-five years and I have the right to expect you to pay full attention to my demands. You must be clean and tidy. Most of all I require punctuality! Is that understood?'

I tried to be all of these things, and Miss Weller introduced me to the files. I thought the system marvellous and expressed my admiration. Whereupon Miss Weller called me 'simple minded' and implied as much in her subsequent sarcastic treatment of me, as she exaggerated her instructions in a slow malicious manner. This behaviour carried on for a couple of weeks and, while doing my best to please her, I could not pierce her obvious aversion to me.

One day Miss Weller informed me that I was to be promoted. She was arranging the tea tray for Mr Clerk himself, with an elegant silver service. I was to be allowed to carry the tray to the door of Mr Clerk's room, where I would hand it over and then go about my business. I adjusted the position of the teapot and carefully picked up the tray.

'Not so much as a thumbprint is required,' she cried, snatching the tray and examining the teapot in a flurry. 'Oh you idiot,' she exclaimed as she replaced the tray upon the table and wiped away an invisible mark.

'You may now carry the tray and follow me.'

I remained still.

Miss Weller snorted. 'Stupid girl! Go on, pick it up then!'

The Devil seized me, for I suddenly raised it up and crashed it to the floor. She screamed and grabbed me by my hair, but I pushed her away and just looked at the panting and raging Miss Weller with utter disdain. She dashed out of the room in a flood of tears, and I was left alone.

After a while one of the smart young men popped his head into the post room. He was smiling.

'Miss Hughes, I'm sorry about all the palaver, you're for the high jump I'm afraid. Have to see the great man himself!'

'High jump?'

'The sack, my dear. Kaput, finito! Lost your job! One thing I'd like to say, little lady. We've all been pleased with your kind considerations. I think you're jolly nice. Chin up, good luck to you! Bye-bye!' And he was gone.

Perhaps half an hour later the same young man quietly opened the door and beckoned me with his finger. I followed him in silence to the door of Mr Clerk. The young man, grinning, drew his thumb across his throat and then held it upright, and whispered: 'Nil desperandum!' and knocked on the door.

A high piping voice from within called me to enter. In a large armchair sat an incredibly shrunken old man with large eyes that seemed to catch the light. His hands clasped in front of him supported his chin.

'Miss Hughes.' His eyes flashed over me. 'I'm sorry I haven't had the privilege of meeting you before, and that our association must needs be brief.'

He picked up an envelope. 'I have here your wages.' He reached over the desk for another envelope. 'And here a packet in lieu of notice.'

He then gave me a brilliant smile, took out his wallet, opening it slowly, and produced a large crisp white note.

'And here is five pounds for extreme courage in the line of duty! I would not have dared. We are all terrified of poor Miss Weller!'

Then he rose, circled the expansive desk, gently took my arm and steered me to the door.

'Miss Hughes, my card!' He tucked it into my hand, in which the money was still clutched.

'If ever I can help you? Good luck, my dear.'

I'd said not a word. I'd even forgotten to thank him.

Miss Cole had been relieved and pleased I'd been placed so well. She was proud to tell her friends that I was with a firm of solicitors. I was sorry that I'd let her down. I decided to get another job with the utmost speed. Not knowing the procedure, but remembering that 'situations vacant' boards were sometimes lodged outside premises, I endeavoured to seek these out.

Taking the number two bus to Victoria, I walked to Trafalgar Square without seeing a single board. So I sat in the sun and shared my sandwiches with the matronly pigeons, fascinated by their occasional odd dancing, and the behaviour of the people who came to feed them.

There were old men who slouched on the benches in an attitude of deflated boredom with unseeing eyes. Now and then one would stoop to pick up a cigarette end or shift his position and I wondered at the lives of these men and what happened to them in winter. The more I observed them, the sadder I felt that they should seem so dulled and so ignored. I left the square, shrugging off an obscure feeling of guilt.

I then approached a couple of the larger stores in Oxford Street where I hoped to find a position as a sales lady. I was laughed at in one. In another a perhaps more kindly woman directed me to gaze at myself in a store mirror, motioning an assistant to join me. What I saw was a smartly turned out doll-like creature, with a pale blank face, and myself, dustily shabby, my hair in a mess, my too long gym-slip dragged off the shoulder with the weight of the scruffy satchel. I just laughed, as did the woman who suggested that I went to an employment exchange.

I dared not tell Miss Cole that I had been sacked and I spent that day and the rest of the week around the streets and museums. My new-found affluence had me paying homage to the cinema, or treating myself to a ride on a train, even spending a day at Brighton. Thus I amused myself until it was time to go home, arriving at the usual time.

Half way through the next week, still unable to find work, I developed a temperature and was found out. Miss Cole was absolutely furious. She had telephoned the solicitors to say that I was unwell, and had spoken to Miss Weller. Miss Cole insisted that I write a letter of apology, and my adamant refusal caused dismay and cries of 'Deceitful child!' The resulting sad silence strained our friendship.

Finally I secured a position, and started as a junior inspector at a local electro-plating factory. This I found quite enjoyable, especially when I progressed to the buffing machines, for I liked working with my hands. The people I worked with were kind and above the roar of the machines wittily commented about life generally, so that I felt most comfortable in their company. The initial hint of antagonism I sensed, perhaps triggered by the

154

way I spoke with Mummy's perfect diction, quickly dissipated when I proved my willingness to work hard. Before long I was totally accepted and had become part of the team.

Overlooking the works there was an office. Those who worked thus elevated received more money for a shorter stint, and plainly regarded us as factory-floor types. Perhaps they were envious of our cheerful spirits. I didn't much care to be considered so low, yet I never had any desire to join those up there, nor did I, unlike some of my colleagues, loathe the better off.

Several weeks later, Miss Cole informed me that she would soon have to give up her house. It seemed that she had mortgaged it to the hilt for the sake of her girls. One by one the students left us, successfully going on to higher education or fine positions. Now it was just the two of us. I was very sad to contemplate leaving her, for I had grown immensely fond of dithering, dear Miss Cole. She had long since forgiven me and still believed, despite my 'awful' job with those 'rough' people, that I had some potential.

Once more Miss Cole urgently renewed her efforts to save me. She would plead earnestly that my quick and alert mind could be used in the service of the Lord, instead of (just as easily) for the depths of depravity . . . One moment her prayers elevated me to celestial heights, and the next implied that I was already on a downward path.

In the meantime, in my first week at the factory, the war had ended. Apart from a brief prayer with Miss Cole and a celebration at the factory, which I was forbidden to attend, it seemed a non-event. There were no newspapers and no wireless in the house to stimulate my interest. It was the impending hereafter that concerned Miss Cole, and she sighed away the subject of the recent world conflict: 'There will be wars and rumours of wars, et cetera!'

Miss Cole loved odd cults. She took me to the Woman's Protestant Truth Society, where Roman Catholicism was violently denounced, and to the British Israelites, where a chap with dyed hair pointed to several charts proving that the British people were really the lost tribes of Israel. He showed great enthusiasm and was most amusing, completely captivating Miss Cole with his thin evidence. Every evening we would do the 'I believe, help Thou mine unbelief!' routine, with such passion that I began to wonder if the prayer was not for herself!

It was almost time to leave, and I accompanied a rather tired Miss Cole to the Croydon offices again. She glowingly pleaded that I had undergone a complete change, and that I would now become a worthy citizen. The awful man I had so dreaded to encounter was absent. The outcome of the interview was that George, my stepfather, was to be made my legal guardian and that I was to reside with him. I found that acceptable.

In my last days under Miss Cole's guardianship, Dorothy suddenly arrived on the arm of a tall, taut, young man, announcing that the Lord wished them to be married. At first I stared at her in disbelief, then we tearfully embraced to the obvious disapproval of Dorothy's Thomas who rigidly parted us. Observing him closely, I found him strangely wooden. He eyed Dorothy with a bird-like anxiety, with not one hint of affection in his regard. Suddenly I felt extreme alarm that my sweet and now pretty sister was to marry this awful man.

When I managed to spend a few brief minutes alone with Dorothy, I begged her not to go through with it. But all too soon Thomas dragged her away, with me crying after her, 'Don't do it, Dorothy, please don't.'

Miss Cole showed no uneasiness. Thomas was on the wireless most evenings in his native Switzerland preaching the Gospel, and she assured me that it was a great honour for Dorothy to have been so chosen. So she tried to comfort me, for I cried bitterly, protesting that the fellow had given me the creeps.

It was time to leave Miss Cole, and I was left in no doubt as to the affection between us. We hugged each other and then she said, earnestly: 'You strange child, I must tell you, if I could have had a daughter, for all your faults, I would have chosen you.'

FOURTEEN

Grief

Images of chaotic life with my mother flashed into my head on my way home.

For the time I had been with Miss Cole my mind had blotted out past miseries. The fact that I'd heard nothing at all from my mother did not surprise me. With some feelings of dismay, I realised that I had not really thought of her. Some episode, seemingly buried in oblivion for I could not remember it, had caused our separation. Now I was briefly filled with dread as I viewed my immediate future with some trepidation. Then I sang songs in my head and, before long, I felt my courage rising within me to face whatever the future held.

George was already standing under the clock in Victoria Station, where it was arranged we should meet.

He warmly greeted me and said that my mother was 'a little better', and that things had improved. But I had no illusions as I looked up into his pinched white face. His pain-ridden eyes avoided my quizzical gaze, and there was a weariness about him that spelled out the situation.

'Home' was wherever they happened to be. We arrived to find my mother unpacking and mess all over the newly acquired flat. She looked astonishingly attractive and greeted me in an off-hand, guarded fashion, but within the hour she had thrown off her elegant suit, pulled off her corset, and was in her bed screaming instructions for the placing of her paraphernalia around the flat. I raced around, anticipating her demands, arranging her trifles and treasures.

'My sweet clever girl, how I've missed you!'

She gave me one of her brilliant smiles and held open her arms. A lump came to my throat and I was about to abandon all my reservations, but she continued:

'Oh God! I've been shut up with this *worm*! This slow-witted *twit*!'

The awful words filled me with dismay. I glanced at George, but he had turned away, choosing to ignore the hurtful remarks. Then my eyes fell upon her discarded clothing which I retrieved from the floor, and with it the vision, just a moment ago, of her looking so splendid. As I gently folded her attire, a brief flash of the dream of a normal mother passed through me. I wept and involuntary tears appeared in darkened spots upon her silk blouse.

'Christ-all-bloody-mighty,' she exploded, and added urgently, 'I'm *joking*, my sweet! *Joking*, aren't I, George? Come, give your Mummy a kiss,' she said petulantly as she shuffled with the bedclothes.

I turned my back, pretending to be busy, and wiped away my tears.

'Oh well, tra-la-la, suit yourself. Don't tell me that you've turned into a young madam!'

George confided in whispers that my mother was very ill, that frequent haemorrhages depleted her strength, that kidney trouble made her appear excessively fat at times. Almost certainly, she suffered from high blood pressure. He had obtained the information from a customer, a doctor, who frequented the dive where he now worked.

Saint or sucker? I couldn't make George out, nor the reason he stayed with her. Almost no words came from him and he seemed to be terrified to be caught talking to me. More than once my mother had screamed vile abuse at us for discussing her.

I spent my days looking after her, relieving poor George of the task which was often fraught with sudden danger. Occasionally, in the night, noises would come from their bedroom that would suggest that George had been hurt. I began to wish she would die, and I would dream of sticking a knife in her, of pushing her under a bus, until I started up from my sleep in terror and felt myself on the brink of madness, too.

My mother's rages became more frequent, and her eyes never lost that glazed look of alert madness. Now she spoke often of death, the thought of which positively terrified her. Each outburst left her more deflated, and a fear that her food was poisoned meant that she slowly starved. Sometimes she would plead piteously that we would forgive her violent outbursts, that evil powers beyond herself were killing her. She would beg us not to desert her.

I was often dreadfully afraid of what she might do to George or indeed myself. The fears were well grounded, for once more, at night, I saw my mother bending over me, not with a knife, but speaking a strange language and chanting wildly. With my heart thumping I slowly eased myself off the bed and slid underneath, close to the cool wall. Then my mother's voice rose screaming that 'they'd' taken me. She wailed agonisingly and repeatedly called out my name.

I told George that I would have to leave. I could no longer bear this way of living. It made me want to die. But the thought of leaving her made me feel enormously guilty, so, helpless and hopeless, I stayed.

Then it happened one day that my mother suddenly got dressed, put an untidy slash of lipstick across her deathly-pale face, and went out. I had been powerless, too afraid even to try to stop her, and I spent the next few hours with a deep sense of anxiety.

A knock at the door realised my fears. A policeman stood there with the news that my mother had collapsed near Hyde Park Corner and the doctors at the hospital required her family to go there at once.

Racing to the hospital, after first contacting George, my thoughts were that Mother was dying. Why else would the policeman have called for her family? I shrugged away grief, feeling mostly a sense of enormous relief as I mounted the stairs and pictured her lying wan and peaceful.

As I dashed into the ward, I was held back. I pushed past the nurse to see my mother gagged and surrounded by nurses and doctors. She was red-faced and panting. And *Mummy*! Oh, those terrified eyes! They injected her and slowly removed the gag. She was conscious but couldn't move. Her eyes pleaded with me, but I felt frozen inside.

George arrived and the doctors were whispering to him.

'... certified now ... paranoid schizophrenic ... could kill ... dangerous ... duty!'

'I can't! I can't do it!' said George hopelessly and staggered away.

'I can! She's my *mother*! I'll sign!' I cried.

The white-coated men looked at each other and then handed me the pen.

I turned to Mummy.

She was mouthing something.

'I will die! Don't! I will die!'

Her words cut into me, but I grabbed at the pen and signed a bold definite signature. Then I turned and ran out and down the stairs and ran and ran. Over and over the thought came to me. *I have killed her! I have killed her! I have killed her.*

Reaching home, I flung myself upon her bed knowing that she

was gone forever. That I would never again hear the beautifully modulated tones of her voice or listen to her low sweet singing, nor see the flash of amusement in her expressive eyes, hear her merry laugh, nor notice the way she could cock a snook at pompousness in the most vulgar manner and immediately transform herself into .a believable portrait of imperious grandeur.

For all her violence, wicked cunning and sometimes evil tongue, I had loved her, and had tried to understand her anguish. In her moments of sanity, I had recognised My Mother of The Letters. She had been the most magnificent, the most real, the most wonderful person I had ever met.

In a paroxysm of grief, I lit a fire in the grate and tearfully burned everything that had been hers. The contents of the tin box, her papers and all her writings. Mummy's sweet shoes, clothes, hairbrushes, make-up, her comb, perfume. The flames leapt up the chimney fit to set the house on fire. So I carried on until I could not immediately find another thing that had belonged to her. Then I lay on her bed and sobbed myself to sleep.

The putting on of a light woke me. George had returned from work. He surveyed the scene silently, then offered to make me a cup of tea. He made no comment on what I had done, and when, a little later, I emerged from a comforting bath, the fire-place was swept clean.

After packing a few things, including the brass ornaments, George and I left the flat and found a couple of rooms in Soho.

George had lost his job, or rather, he had walked out of it, for the club and the goings-on in it sickened him. We sold the brass for five shillings a piece to a bow-fronted antique shop called Juno's. I was pleased to see them go; I could not bear to look upon the familiar and once-loved pieces, and now the money came in useful.

George was ill and withered, and seemed to be in a state of shock. He had treated my mother with infinite tolerance and gentleness. When she ranted maliciously against him, he showed no reactive anger but, as she had deteriorated, so had he. Barely past forty, he looked haggard and old.

The two of us talked only of the weather and seemed never to look at each other. We were both horribly wounded. And overwhelmingly guilty.

We never mentioned Mummy.

With both of us feeling so low, George decided that we should go to the cinema. The 'B' film passed, music heralded the oncoming news. A man's voice kept up a running, breathless commentary on various items using the same urgency of tone. Then, almost without a pause, dreadful pictures of the Nazi horrors from the concentration camps in Germany were flashed on to the screen. First a mountain of shoes, shabby and well-worn, with the impressions still upon them of the feet of the people who had shaped them. A mute, stark, searing agony of devastation followed. A Dante's Inferno, animated in living skeletons of humanity, squatting listlessly in the shade of great heaps of hollow-eyed skeletal corpses that seemed to stretch to the heavens in a curse. The voice carried on ' . . . many millions . . .'

Something happened in my head. I stood up. 'No! No! No!' I yelled, and stumbled out.

In the foyer, I removed my shoes, under some irresistible impulse. Barefoot, I ran home.

Fear overwhelmed me. 'This happened now! This must be the final calamity . . . this happened now!' The ghastly scenes would not leave me. I felt threatened. This surely was hell upon earth? It was unbelievable! Unbelievable! But I'd seen it, the vision stayed with me, and I couldn't endure it.

I shouted out: 'Everything is finished! All are damned! This evil will swallow us all!'

So my mind was racked. In the space of a traumatic week, I had signed Mummy's death warrant and those terrible scenes of awful devastation had been thrust upon me in the cinema. My senses had simply been engulfed by emotion. I succumbed to a fever, which I hoped would take my life away. I wished for oblivion. The world was too terrifying, too empty a place.

George hovered about me. Slowly the fever abated, and I was left in a subdued state. It seemed that the light had gone out of my life. The food George offered nauseated and choked me. I knew that I must snap out of my misery, but I knew not how.

It occurred to me that I must order my thinking and I sent George for a Bible. In my confusion, I was asking the vital question: 'Who and what am I?' For weeks I pored over the Book, seeking new answers as I thumbed my way through half-remembered passages.

I thought of the atrocities done in the name of God; of the law of the jungle; of how I myself had seen the sufferings of small animals and insects. A Divine overseer who toyed with all forms of life on earth so cruelly must be baser than the meanest man. What of the enormous tragedy that had afflicted Mummy? Did He create disease? What for?

My feelings and emotions were mixed indeed and my search for truths inhibited by my incredible ignorance in all spheres. I felt as nothing.

I knew that there were people in this country who could perpetrate the horrors of the Nazi concentration camps if ever the situation arose where violence and force overrode just interpretation of the law. I had heard the words of Jesus interpreted with love and with vile damnation. Justice and judgement seemed two ends of a rope, the one a lifeline, the other a noose.

It dawned upon me that God must be man's invention. There seemed to be no evidence otherwise, and therefore I was free of the slavery of an idea that had no substance. And goodness? Goodness was worth pursuing for its own sake, as were knowledge and wisdom.

Slowly I came out of the morass, and out of the devastating inner feelings of utter desolation. I concluded that there was no God; that I had just this one life, somewhat sadly acknowledging a loss of eternal life; that there was no damnation; that heaven and hell could be found here, on earth; that I must start my life again, and that somehow I would have to educate myself. Too late for school, and not knowing where to begin, I resolved to seek wisdom.

George, by this time, had found another job. He left at lunchtime and returned after midnight. He would cook a late breakfast automatically, since he had always waited upon my mother. Then together we'd tidy our Soho rooms which were light and airy. We wouldn't talk much and I liked him for that. He was peaceful and the silence held no awkwardness. Often we found no need for words, but communicated intuitively.

It was then I decided to call George 'Pops'. I told the landlady that he was my father. Previously I had refrained from calling him anything.

Soon I was out and about again. My cheerful spirit returned and my self-centred concerns ended. Indeed I had become aware that Pops seemed to earn very little money and owned insufficient clothing, so it was necessary that I find myself a post of some sort.

Thus it was that I found myself in a sheet-tin-cutting factory, working on a compressed steam-operated guillotine, cutting out the printed forms of Tate & Lyle golden syrup tins. These machines were highly dangerous, no doubt causing nervousness in some of the women. We would whip great sharp-edged sheets of tin about as we fed the machine, guiding and supporting the sheets with our stomachs. Then we'd slide a leg under the bench to a distant pedal to activate the cutting blade. The resulting noise was shattering.

All this pandemonium was supervised by two men who passed the time of day while we worked hell-for-leather. For this, they were paid twice the wages of the most skilled of us. They were the maintenance men, who slouched around with an oil-can, offering obscene comments as they leered their way through our oddly spaced benches. I daresay they had some simple skills that any of us, given the opportunity, could have mastered.

In this very stressful situation, tempers ran high among the women. One lunch break, a fight broke out between two girls wielding coat hangers. Their screams were accompanied by cat-calls from the others, including the men, who gathered round. Sickened by witnessing this upset and put off by a certain hostility over my accent, by my cut hands and a nasty gash on my knee which one of the oafs found amusing, I walked away.

Pops had been horrified that I had found such a job and he was much relieved by the knowledge that I'd chucked it. It occurred to me how hard, and in what appalling conditions, some people had to work for not much more money than kept them just above the breadline. I thought about the shattering noise of the factory. Inhaling the lumps of oily smut that wafted above the presses perhaps accounted for the pallor of the women, who constantly blew dirt from their noses. The meagre filthy lunch facilities forced them to eat perched upon tables alongside the presses, for there were no chairs.

My next appointment was selling shoes in a large shop in Victoria Street. I had a love of flat, sensible and well-made shoes with plenty of room so that one could stride out well supported. Many of the shoes on sale there were so narrow, so pointed and the heels so high, that I could not imagine the wearing of them to be anything but torture. The chance to scan so many feet enabled me to see the relationship between shoes and posture. It started as a game, for there were many idle hours. I watched women mincing in and out of the shop and thought vaguely of the old Chinese custom of foot-binding. Observing men striding past the windows, walking freely as I did, I wondered if they consciously felt the joy of it, as I did.

Not aware of the danger, for there was no warning, I would frequently twiddle my toes in a wonderful x-ray machine, fascinated with the marvels of the animated skeleton of my foot. Another member of the staff would sometimes condescend to lend me her foot for better observation, while she cast her eyes up to the ceiling and emited sighs of utter boredom.

After some months, I was suddenly sacked. It seemed that I had too often impertinently advised ladies that they should not purchase this and that pair of shoes.

Pops developed some trouble with his forearm; it had started to hurt him, a definite dent appeared in the bone and now it was encased in plaster. The unsightly cast, and his incapacity to fulfil certain duties, persuaded his boss to dispense with him. He was able to claim a small amount of money, but it was insufficient to cover even the rent, and we had no savings.

I had turned fifteen and was grateful to Pops for the peace his gentle nature had allowed me. I was aware that I should show some sense of responsibility, but the sun was casting shorter shadows, and I yearned once more for the countryside.

With some difficulty, for the suggestion filled him with doubts, I persuaded Pops that we should 'hit the road'. We gave up our rooms, leaving our few possessions with the landlady who kindly arranged for a friend of hers to lend us a tent. Soon we were off, thumbing a lift on the Bayswater Road. I was in my element, but Pops was full of fears. He believed in hanging on to security and safety.

We managed to get as far as Cornwall where we camped on a

piece of scrubby land near the beach, eating once a day at a government-subsidised restaurant. Luck was with us, for Pops got himself an agreeable job as a deck-chair ticket collector. The fellow holding this fine position had been fired on the spot. He had literally fallen down on the job in an alcoholic stupor. Pops and I had been stretched out on the sand and had witnessed this. I had nudged Pops into an instant application. The boss shook his head, eyeing Pops's arm, but I cried, 'We've three between us!' and that was that.

It was one of those rare, long, hot summers and we both seemed to bloom in the warm, lazy atmosphere. I spent most of the day poring over the wonders on the edge of the sea, scuffing my bare feet through the sands. Many hours were spent beach-combing, and we found all sorts of things, including the odd coin.

Our boss, a jocular man, was exceedingly pleased with himself, having found such a capable pair to work for so little. He in turn was employed by a private firm and was responsible for many tasks which he slowly loaded on to us, offering no further renumeration. When I protested, for Pops would not, the boss would sigh and suggest sadly that perhaps he should find a man more capable, knowing that we had little alternative except to comply with his demands.

One day he suggested to me that I could help Pops by retrieving discarded deck-chair tickets and reissuing them. We could split the proceeds between us. I gave him a look of utter indignation, to which he responded by telling me that he was just testing our honesty.

This suggestion I immediately put into practice, thus enhancing our meagre income without letting the boss in on our proceeds.

Despite my search for goodness, I would fall into old habits now and then. Occasionally I stole cigarettes, for we both smoked heavily, and Pops seemed jittery without them. I would tell him that I had found the money in the sands – sometimes I had.

Time passed and I became more aware of the personalities of people. Here, idling on the sands, faces lost that tense, harassed expression, common on the streets of London. Like all things, people seemed to expand under the kindly, undemanding radiance of the sun.

Even Pops got his typically English R.A.F. handsome looks back again. The years seemed to roll off him; he became less nervous and more self-assured. People were constantly amazed that a man of his distinguished bearing and manner was in such reduced circumstances.

Almost at the end of the season, a family befriended us and Pops was offered a job as the sole porter in a block of flats just off Baker Street. It was too good an opportunity to let go.

Reluctantly, and with excellent references from the boss, we set off for London and 'civilisation'.

This had been my happiest summer and was to be my last episode of vagabond life.

FIFTEEN

Freedom

It was still August, and no sooner had I arrived on the hot, dusty streets of London, than I found myself once more longing for the countryside. Pops, kept constantly busy, was happy enough ministering to the needs of the wealthy, and was fully employed with little time for my company, not that he was ever very communicative.

Remembering the sight of the girls in the Land Army and admiring their breeches a little enviously, I applied unsuccessfully to join their ranks. I was, however, informed of a scheme called 'Lend a hand on the land'. At fifteen-and-a-half, I was too young, but my enthusiasm and the shortage of willing labour encouraged the organisers to accept me.

In three days I was on a train to Norfolk accompanied by a group of young people, my head filled with romantic notions of an idyllic destination.

The farmer, a tall miserable bag of bones of few words, sourly greeted us at the station. We were herded on to the back of an open lorry and driven bumpily to our objective.

The farm turned out to be miles away from anywhere, a massive acreage of potatoes, cabbage and sugar beet, no animals at all and no farmer's wife. The rough accommodation consisted of two windswept sheds that divided the sexes and provided little comfort. We dropped off our bags and, without so much as a cup of tea, were taken to a bleak field, each armed with a hoe, to weed the biggest cabbage patch imaginable. We were placed at the beginning of a row that stretched to the horizon; I speedily distanced myself from the others, and softly sang into the gentle breeze. Within the hour, four of the group went off on foot, back to the station and home, but most of us were made of sterner stuff.

The work was hard and by the evening we were exhausted. The food, brought to us by the farmer in a truck, was awful and, for some, too little. Sometimes we'd gather about a fire in the open to sing or chat. Five young men, full of fun, had come from Sweden. They brightly discussed many subjects in perfect English. I watched and listened, finding out about my ignorance and never opening my mouth. I was used to a solitary existence and sometimes I felt uneasy in the company of these young people.

After the weeding of the cabbages, we followed a tractor digging up potatoes (spud-bashing) filling baskets which were later loaded on to the lorry. The Swedes soon developed a loathing for the farmer and drove him to distraction by refusing to speak English. They learned to sabotage the ancient tractor by putting a potato into the upturned exhaust pipe; then, when the farmer went in search of a mechanic, removing the potato and driving the machine madly around the farm.

Unexpectedly I was offered the privilege of a turn, and, with a little instruction, I was driving the tractor full pelt up and over the gently rolling fields. Then, suddenly, four of the young people strung out in front of me, playfully daring me to run them down. Not knowing how to stop, I was forced to make a wild turn and brought the thing over on top of me. The tractor roared and spluttered bearing down upon me while I braced all my muscles in an attempt to stop the heat and noise grinding me into oblivion. It seemed an age passed before it was rolled away from me and I became conscious of searing pain.

Terror was reflected in the faces bending over me. Blood poured from my mouth and I was unable to stand. The farmer was nowhere to be seen, so they gathered me up and carried me to the roadside to thumb a lift to a hospital. While we waited, we ascertained that I had damaged my jaw and perhaps broken my ankle. A car was hailed madly. It slowed, surveyed our muddy gang, then pelted off again. Then a Rolls Royce came into view and I was dangled as if dead in the arms of the tallest Swede. The Rolls stopped, we piled in and the car glided away, taking me to the hospital in great style.

My ankle was fractured, and they put it in plaster. My jaw was badly bruised and I required some dentistry on a back tooth. Sadly, for I had just begun to communicate a little shyly with the Swedes who suddenly seemed to take to me, I had to return to London.

Enforced idleness gave me an opportunity to read the detective novels of Raymond Chandler. The choice of Pops, they were followed by the works of Dennis Wheatley and a host of similar books, including the morbid horrors of Edgar Allen Poe. Dear Pops was amazed at the speed at which these novels were read and discarded. In fact I was reading with relentless persistence in order to blot out sudden thoughts of Mummy, who perhaps was not dead. My anxiety mounted. Where was she? Had I buried her alive? I had to ask Pops. I had to see her. The worry took my appetite away. Pops eyed my untouched food with anxious looks, but made no comment. Finally I broached the subject, hesitantly, for Pops was horribly distressed at the mere mention of her name.

In less than a week, I was on my way to an asylum in Epsom, where eventually I was shown into what appeared to be a large dining-room. Following the pointed finger of an impatient nurse, I could not see my mother among the quiet forms that dotted the room. The nurse took my arm and marched me forward.

'There. Can't you see? There.'

We stopped in front of a thin, white-haired woman standing gently smoothing the edge of a table and staring unseeingly at a blank wall.

I gazed at her unbelievingly. This could not be Mummy!

'No . . .' I began.

'She'll be all right.' The nurse's voice softened. 'She's had electric shock treatment. She was very bad when she came here, but she's calm now. She's a good girl now.'

Resisting the urge to cry out, for I now recognised her, I lifted my mother's hand; it was cool and limp and thin. Her hands had always been warm. I found myself gently rubbing it.

'Mummy! It's me, Marian!'

There was no response. I felt a desperate grief. She looked so dehumanised.

'Mummy! Mummy! What have they done to you?'

I felt myself being dragged away by the nurse. 'Now don't you go upsetting everybody! We've done our best for her, see?'

Nodding bitterly, almost blinded by tears, I turned and was out of the place. Despite the pain in my leg, I ran to the station. To see Mummy like that! A living death! Her hair white! What was electric shock treatment?

Pops did not ask about my mother. But I read his expression.

'She's fine. She didn't know me.'

I searched Pops's face.

'What is electric shock treatment?'

A slight gesture, as he turned away, seemed to say, 'I don't want to know.'

The next day I went to the local library. I could not find a proper description anywhere. Electric shock was dimly explained: they didn't know how it worked; it seemed for some it just did.

I secreted the book to read that chapter again and again, and that other bit on schizophrenia. The book was six years old. I went back and looked for something more up-to-date. Obsessed with finding the cause and a possible cure for my mother's condition I spent many hours seeking, searching through volumes so obscure they seemed almost written in a foreign tongue.

Suddenly my mind was made up: I'd train to be a nurse. Applying at a local hospital I was told that I had to be seventeen. The disappointment must have showed. 'They'd take you at sixteen in a mental hospital and not be so fussy about qualification.' The lady had eyed my strange apparel, and probably hadn't believed my tale of education by private tutor in India.

Gratefully taking the address, a hospital in Virginia Waters, I decided to write nearer my birthday. In the meantime I'd have to learn about human anatomy. So I acquired some books (in the usual manner to which I was accustomed) and spent many hours prodding my own body in wonderment.

I found myself a job, too, in a small building and engineering office near Regent's Park. Thirty shillings a week, to be a junior office clerk. Where the solicitor's office had been rigidly formal, this was friendly, chatty at times and frantically busy. Peals of ribald laughter came from the rooms of the 'chief', as they called him.

Here I heard my first dirty jokes, some of which were beyond my comprehension. I knew the others found me quaint, but they were kind, and appreciated my earnest efforts.

Oh, the magic of the typewriter! Miss Newton would chat and at the same time type reams of tabulated invoices at enormous speed. I vowed that I would master her art. Lunchtimes, I was allowed to play with one of the machines. Laboriously matching my fingers to the right keys, I managed to achieve a moderate skill, undermined only by my appalling efforts at spelling. A rich vocabulary, a patchwork of knowledge enhanced by the Bible, hymns and poetry, made my story of private tuition in India convincing. By now I had been impelled to read the history of that country. The works of Rudyard Kipling had conjured up the most glorious illusion of what my life might have been like in the sprawling military camps of Bangalore. Not that I'd enlarge upon it unless I had to.

The people in the office fascinated me. The younger women's lives revolved around boyfriends, fashion and film stars. Nothing else seemed of interest. I was amazed they felt no urge to enquire into the meaning of life and never questioned their own lives. Nylons, their seams and the shape of their heels, were frequent topics of conversation, and the display of the very latest make-up and clothes brought gasps of envious wonder. I appreciated the gossamer and perfection of some of these items, but the impractical, vulnerable and frail had no place in my wardrobe. I was still barely six stone. My dress was still knickers, vest and rags. As for make-up, I couldn't ever become the scarlet woman of the Proverbs. Make-up seemed a stamp of primitive woad-painting. I was intrigued by the time-consuming art, which included the plucking of eyebrows. It seemed to me that these nice, sweet-smelling girls were on a different plane. They had innocence. No blight on their lives. I had to blot out my blights by creating an infancy in India, a cleaner childhood that would not haunt me with my own unworthiness.

They were always singing the latest songs in this cosy office; I added them to the collection stored in my head. While I was too shy to sing with these confident girls, I'd sing the songs at home.

They had an office party at Christmas, too, and presents. I had my first wrapped-up gift, with my name on it! Bath salts! Two or three grains in my next bath had me wallowing in luxury.

Miss Newton helped me choose little gifts for the others. Sandwiches, tea cakes and singing after work heralded the holiday, and my graduation to invoice typing, and a rise in salary.

So I was happily engaged until the spring.

My application for training as a nurse had been accepted for a probationary period of three months. Clutching my letter, a little tatty from constant reference, I arrived, aged just sixteen, with my small case. I stood on the steps of what had once been a palace. The marbled columns of the grand entrance hall belied the stark economy within.

'Miss Hughes you are one day too late! One day too late! We started yesterday.'

The tutor turned her back. I just stood there in the classroom. She washed down the blackboard, ignoring me. She looked quite old, severe and had a faint down on her upper lip. Her false teeth were too small, too even. Crinkly, iron-grey, bobbed hair clung stickily to her head, reminding me of 1920s magazines. Dark blue uniform and white belt gave her rank.

There were charts all around the walls and a beautiful skeleton dangled from an iron frame. It was like a school. Suddenly I passionately and desperately wanted to go to school.

Determined to hang around, I waited for a long half hour. The tutor moved among the desks putting out books and paper and filling ink wells, then started screeching chalk across the board. At last she turned to me.

'I told you to go!' She looked me up and down fastidiously. 'Visiting day is Sunday. Or are you to be an inmate?'

'I wish to study here,' I said firmly.

She shuffled through the file and found the relevant notes. She closed the file.

'Miss Hughes was definitely dismissed yesterday.'

A noise was heard outside the classroom, and in a moment a group of young girls, dressed in yellow gingham short-sleeved frocks with starched white aprons, appeared and made their way in silence to their desks. There was one empty place; I deposited my case unobtrusively and sat upon the empty seat. Thus I listened to my first lesson on anatomy.

The lecture lasted for two hours. At the end of it, the tutor handed out a questionnaire. I thought she would pass me by, but she smiled faintly and gave me one, too.

It was a hard life. Up at six in the morning, making beds, cleaning up patients, combing their hair amid cries or amazingly intelligent conversations.

The beds were packed close together with no lockers between them. My bed-making made an impression. During the days that followed I called upon the skills I had learned all those years ago in the old Orphanage.

Eight o'clock, breakfast; nine o'clock, shepherding the patients in the grounds or more ward-cleaning; half past ten, cleaning our own rooms; eleven o'clock, the lecture of the day; twelve-thirty, lunch; one-thirty, compulsory games at the tennis courts or swimming or physical exercises. I was forced into the netball team. Two-thirty, back on the wards. And so the day went, until eight-thirty. Most students found the routine exhausting and were slow to keep up with tutors' demands, especially those who spent their evenings going out and about. Doors were locked at ten o'clock bedtime, but relationships still developed between female and male staff or local lads who would quickly appraise the new arrivals on their Sunday ventures into the town. A few girls were sent packing, after clumsy efforts to get back in at night or falling asleep in lectures.

The plight of some patients worried me. One woman had been incarcerated for forty years. While she was not particularly intelligent, I could see nothing wrong with her.

'God sent me here to care for these poor things. It was a punishment,' she said.

'A punishment? What for?' I asked.

'It's between me and God!'

Nothing more could be got out of her. It seemed that, while in service, she had been seduced and made pregnant by her master who had had her hidden away to spend her life in this institution. She had been taught, many years ago, to be grateful for God's mercy to her!

Some of the patients were really deranged. There were the posers, with limbs permanently and tortuously shortened or stretched, and others with manifestations of hysteria, equally distressing. Some just sobbed all day or would cry out to invisible bodies. There were those who seemed normal, but would suddenly become violent; once I was struck with a nail, held merely in the patient's hand, with such force that it pierced my arm to the bone.

The situation of the patients saddened me, yet I could not imagine what more could be done for them. Many were lost with no hope for a cure. Tragic, and forgotten by the community, and conveniently shut away. Their basic needs were attended to by saintly women or by cheery nurses who treated them like naughty children. I occasionally heard exasperated reprimands, but never saw any cruelty.

The three months seemed to go quickly. I passed the preliminary examination satisfactorily, but the experience cured me of any desire to nurse, and I left.

The tutor, now charming, expressed some regret.

Pops was evidently delighted to see me; usually a man of few words, he made a fuss of me and insisted on a trip to the music hall to celebrate my return. Later, over a meal, we discussed the possibility of saving up to go to India for an extended holiday. He noticed that I read books on the subject, and he knew I longed to see the places my mother had so often talked of. So, we made a pact. We'd both work hard for a year, saving every penny, then travel. First India, then who knows!

August brought a sudden burst of sunshine. I became restless and was soon off once more in search of the countryside. The 'Lend a hand on the land' campaign had all but fizzled out, but I was put in touch with a group of five going to Devon to pull flax.

This time it was a proper farm, with animals, including chickens, dogs and cats. The farmer's wife could have stepped out of a children's picture book. Buxom and rosy, she decided that 'these Lunnen chillern needed fillin' up!' Great spreads were evident at every mealtime on a table seating eighteen souls.

It was a happy, slovenly atmosphere. Nothing too clean, which sometimes made me feel a mite dismayed. Great fun was had in the fields, the work was hard and everybody fell asleep early.

An ancient aunt of the farmer showed me the secrets of the various processes of making linen from flax. Since a girl, she had pulled, soaked, beaten and woven the flax, and always retained her own patch, still producing cloth for the family needs. One of the hands informed me that the growing of flax might have died out on the farm had it not been needed during the war. The flax supplemented the shipments of jute from India, from which they made the millions of sandbags that had been used throughout the country.

Everybody on the farm seemed old, over fifty, and, feeling at ease in their company, I would listen for hours to the stories of their lives. I would admire treasured handicrafts, from lace to hand-made shoes, and such things as farm implements, fashioned delicately and forged at a neighbouring smithy.

Clambering about an old shed which had been untouched for forty years (so said the farmer's aunt), I unearthed wonderful artifacts, to the delight of the old lady who chuckled happily, relating the history of each item.

The main industry of the area was cider. Our farm possessed an enormous acreage of scrubby, gnarled apple trees dotted with small yellow fruit. These were soon to be hand picked and taken to the great cider presses. On this labour-intensive farm, they still had magnificent Shire horses to pull the long trailers. Even these trailers were made on the farm. A visiting wheel-wright maintained the wood and iron-clad wheels, also helping the resident hooper with the making of the cider barrels. I observed that both of these trades, and the shoeing of the horses, depended on the art of the blacksmith.

The inter-related life of the local community seemed to centre around the farm. With other visitors, such as men from the Ministry of Food, and elderly representatives of the upper-crust slyly begging extra rations, a variety of colourful conversations abounded around the vast kitchen table.

When it rained, I helped with the scrubbing and cleaning of the cider vats which still smelled headily from the previous season. Local women began to arrive, often with their own crop of apples, offering their labour in exchange for the processing. Sometimes they would sell the apples for next to nothing when great argument, fist-shaking and often tears spelled out how much the old farmer was cheating them. Some came to help pick the farm crop and would be occupied, until the weather improved, repairing baskets and making string from the flax, with an ease I envied.

Once, out on the flax fields, for the weather had turned hot and still, I developed a great thirst. I had forgotten to bring any water and, encouraged by the old hands, I downed a large ladleful of the distasteful rough cider, pulling a face as I did so.

'Weren't so bad, eh?' chuckled one amused old fellow. 'Go on, 'ave another!'

I declined.

'Too much for you then, Missie?' He turned to the others. 'She's a soft'un!'

I took the challenge and, like a simpleton, I downed another, and another. My head started to spin. I drank another and suddenly my legs could not mount the stubble in the field. My efforts were accompanied by shrieks of laughter. Mine? My hand slid down the handle of the ladle as I guided the elusive bowl to my lips with great determination. Then the sun went out and I lay spinning, slowly being sucked into the earth.

Hours later I awoke to find myself in the shade of baled flax, my head filled with pulsating pain and shame, and I retched and vomited in the unescapable view of the men who cruelly laughed at my plight.

For two days I felt dreadfully ill. The nauseating smell of the cider invaded every area of the farm. Never! Never will I ever touch the stuff again!

The others who had come to the farm with me had long since left for London. The old farmer had parted with pain with the pittance due to the young people. He suffered severely from meanness when it came to money. His wife was quite the opposite, but she had to fight for her own. Occasionally she'd threaten to beat her husband, picking up fearsome objects, and he'd cower submissively, handing over money which she would snatch triumphantly from his hand calling him 'an old skinflint!' Then the farmer would rush outside, charging about the farm shaking one hand behind him as if seeking to swat a pest.

It seemed that he owed many of the elderly retainers money over many years. Since they were housed and fed, he saw wages as an unreasonable addition. He would part with money 'on account of what he owed', and for tobacco, but only after petulant rantings. Once, I witnessed him as he closed his eyes and put his fingers in his ears, shouting 'Ra! Ra! Ra!', while a

181

poor fellow insisted on a little of his due. His wife laughed at the efforts of others to get their money, never taking up their cause with her husband.

A wet start to the month of October concluded a happy stay at the farm. I left, loving all the inhabitants, for they took to me so well, so kindly. The old farmer twisted in agony and clutched his head with his fists when I tentatively asked for at least my train fare home. I had not the heart to pursue my claim. Pops, eager for my return, wired me the money. I shyly received good-bye kisses from all and sundry.

The farmer's wife made me a present of two pairs of breeches, left behind apparently unappreciatively, even loathingly, by an unwilling member of the Land Army, an organisation still in place after the war. I had been too young to be a Land Girl, but frivolously envied a uniform in which one could run and prance about so freely. With the lovely breeches, and the socks to go with them, plus a bundle of flax from the old aunt for remembrance, I caught the train home.

SIXTEEN

Love

The airiness and tranquillity of the countryside seen from the train from Cornwall contrasted dramatically with the approach to London. Still the devastation appalled and tugged grimly at my soul. Guiltily, I wondered why I'd been judged worthy to live through it. But, as the train ended its journey, the guilty wonderment of survival was instantly dismissed as the business of living was resumed.

At the station I slipped into the ladies' room and changed into my new passion. I emerged from the exotically tiled gleaming brass ornamental lavatories sporting Land Army breeches and khaki socks and caught sight of Pops waiting under the main clock.

'What *have* you got on?'

He looked amused by my get-up as we set off for the premises of his new position in Charing Cross Road. As porter, he had his own two-bedroomed luxury flat over the Phoenix Theatre.

Soon I was working happily with him, cleaning the passages and stairs, mending fuses and running errands. Later I found work that I could do at home.

A little shop in the turning almost opposite sold raffia goods, and required expertly made handicraft articles. I managed to convince them that I'd been making raffia shoes and hats practically all my life. I was provided with materials, for which, in the first instance, I had to pay cost, dubiously given by Pops. As soon as the shop closed, I anxiously studied the goods in the window, before attempting a simple handbag of a design copied from an advertisement. The bag was found to be acceptable and I confidently introduced the idea of raffia lampshades.

The work was poorly paid, but such undemanding occupation employed my hands creatively leaving my mind free to think. I dreamed of the mounting shillings which would result in a passage to India.

My choice of clothing – slacks, shirts and sandals – suited my spirit. I loathed dresses and found them unflattering and uncomfortable for I was very thin. My disposition had long reverted to my normal cheerfulness and I was constantly singing songs, hymns, anything that would lift my soul, and (although I had become terribly shy and avoided people) I felt cleansed from the insanity of the past.

On a bright sunny morning I went in search of Pops's favourite brand of cigarettes, and entered a little café alongside Foyles, the book shop. A hubbub of excited conversation created a veritable din. I joined a line at the counter. An intense argument started in front of me and there were cries of 'Shove on!' behind me. The foursome ahead stood their ground oblivious of the gap seized upon by opportunistic queuers. A shouting match erupted over my head.

I slipped into a vacant seat at the end of a table, the better to observe the seemingly confident girls and men, some in outlandish attire. Each rectangular table sat six people, and a quick glance told me that I had joined five young men. Then I became aware of the conversation at my table.

'What can you expect from these bloody Jews?'

These words startled me. I knew nothing of Jews, but, with

184

the Nazi horrors still fresh in the frightened part of my mind, such a statement, met with smiling enthusiasm, shocked me.

'I beg your pardon,' I said, horrified to feel myself blushing. 'Why do you say "Bloody Jews"?'

Five pairs of eyes turned on me.

'Oh, the Jews are a bloody lot! We should know.' The young man who spoke hid his sniggering smile with his hand.

'But the war?' I stammered, wishing I'd kept my mouth closed. 'Didn't we . . . ? Wasn't there enough of that . . .? You just can't say that . . . we have to stop it!'

Said one gravely: 'Ah! You mean little old Hitler? Well, he was no damn good!' I looked to him with relief but he went on: 'He was incompetent. He didn't finish the job.' Then he guffawed loudly like a donkey, drawing more eyes upon me.

'You are laughing at me!' Humiliation brought tears of anger and I rose abruptly, but the man next to me pulled me back on to the seat.

'Come, we didn't mean to upset you.' He seemed genuinely sorry. Suddenly, he leaned over and kissed me on the cheek. The others roared with laughter at my confusion. I got up and ran from the café, my feelings inexpressible. Then I became aware that the man who had kissed me was following. Now he was jogging alongside and I was surprised that he was so tall.

'Please! Please go away,' I sniffed, but he persisted so I stopped and faced him.

'Really, they didn't mean any harm. You seemed so quaint.' He smiled.

'Quaint? What do you mean by quaint?'

'How old are you?'

'I am nearly seventeen.' Well, I was sixteen-and-a-half precisely.

'I'd have put you down as about thirteen or fourteen.' Smilingly he looked me up and down. 'Where have you been in that get-up?' He tweaked at my breeches.

'Riding,' I lied.

'You can ride a horse?'

'Pretty well,' I lied again, never having been on one.

'Oh, where do you ride?'

'Hyde Park stables.' I'd seen horses there.

'Must cost you a fortune?' He cast his eyes over me speculatively.

'Oh, no,' I quickly replied. I had unwittingly created quite the wrong impression. 'It costs us nothing at all . . . we have friends there!' I was relieved to have got out of that one.

He changed the subject. 'Where do you live?'

'Above the theatre.' I pointed.

He gave a low whistle. 'Must cost at least a tenner a week?'

'My dad's the porter there.'

'Oh, and your mother?'

I hesitated. 'Died in the bombing. I was twelve.'

'That must have been awful!' He sounded genuinely sympathetic. 'Are you English? I seem to detect a slight accent.'

'Oh frightfully,' I said in an upper-crust voice and laughed. 'I spent my childhood in India. You know, British colonial types.'

I suddenly remembered that Pops was waiting for his cigarettes. 'I really ought to be getting back.'

His brown eyes looked smilingly down upon me. 'Do come and have a cup of coffee with me.' I hesitated but his hand gently held my arm and I found myself being led.

As we entered the café, I slipped away with 'I must get some cigarettes.'

'I'll get the coffee. Come back, won't you?' he called.

I'd half a mind to disappear, but in a moment I returned and joined him, lighting a cigarette as I did so.

'You shouldn't smoke. It's bad for you. You're so young.' He looked concerned. 'How long have you been at that?'

'Oh, since I was about twelve.' Then I quickly turned the conversation towards him.

He was twenty-four, his parents originated from Persia but he was born in Egypt. He was brought up in Vienna and his family had come to England in 1936. Now he studied art at St Martin's Art School.

I was surprised that grown people spent their time at school painting pictures, and said as much. My ignorance amazed him, and I confessed that I had never consciously looked at a painting.

'I'll take you to the National Gallery and the Tate. You've heard of them, haven't you?' But he could see that I hadn't. 'Didn't you learn anything at school?'

'A bit, not much.' I said it half-ashamed. 'I really must go now.'

He followed me out of the café and stood for a moment with me on the pavement.

'Will I see you again? I don't even know your name.'

'Marian.'

'I shall call you Maid Marian. My name is Michael, people call me "Mike".'

'I shall call you Michael.'

His hand reached out but I avoided it and skipped away.

I didn't go the short distance home at my usual breakneck speed; lightness pervaded my being, and I wanted to savour the feeling. I could still see his halting gesture as we parted, feel his gentle and strong hand upon my arm, and a sudden awareness swept over me. His moustache? That I would normally have viewed as funny, yet somehow it added to his magnificence.

All this time Pops had waited for his cigarettes. His big blue eyes clouded over with anxiety. As I related joyfully my meeting of my new-found friend and the art students at the café, I detected disapproval creeping into his expression.

He pointed to my raffia work spread out neatly on the table. 'You were to have delivered those this morning.'

A pang of guilt stabbed at me. The clock showed the disap-

pearance of the morning. I had been the most reliable of the out-
workers. Contrite, I gathered the two hats and raced across the
road.

The next few days were spent working furiously, but I took care
to rush my work across the road at the time when most of the
students arrived for a cup of tea before entering the school. I
would stand pretending to gaze at the books in the window of
Foyles, all the while hoping to see the reflection of my friend.

Eventually I plucked up the courage to visit the little café. The
queue at the counter obscured my vision and I didn't spot him
at first, but then I saw him with his arm round a girl. I would
have vanished, but his eyes caught mine and he immediately
rose, extending his hand and motioning to the vacant seat
opposite him. I sat hesitantly and felt myself flush as he introduced those at the table.

All were students, around the age of twenty. They impressed
me with their casual self-assurance and friendliness towards
each other. I reasoned, with a pang, as Michael replaced his arm
round the girl, that she must be his sweetheart.

She seemed so sophisticated. Her nails were long and her rich
brown hair arranged extravagantly on top of her head. I ran my
hand over my own ragged, silky hair and examined my hands,
my short, chipped nails, and I wished I had taken more care of
them. The girl's dress was cut low, revealing her bosom. I clasped my hands together placing my elbows upon the table as it
occurred to me that I had not the slightest sign of development.
Unexpectedly my sister Dorothy's form flashed before me. With
the image of her in Oxford Street came the sad memory that she
hadn't seemed pleased to meet me, so I shook that shapely
apparition from my mind. Up to now I'd revelled in my slim,
streamlined agility. I could jump like a flea and dart and slither
through any crowd like quicksilver, my long blonde hair streak-
ing behind me, and run, just for the joy of it.

Michael was the centre of attention. His gaiety and ability to throw back his head and laugh wholeheartedly contrasted with his rather severe good looks. People of whom I had no knowledge were earnestly discussed and the conversation ranged over many subjects. I took no part, but listened, sharply fascinated.

'Hello, you old bastard!' Michael called to a fellow in the queue at the counter.

It seemed an awful thing to say, but the young man received the greeting warmly, giving Michael a two-handed clasp and plonking a kiss on the nearest girl. I watched him as he made his exit. Thumbs in the air above his head, he danced around a couple on their way into the café, threatening the girl with a kiss and seeming to receive an affectionate thrust from the chap as he skipped past them.

A man was trying to scrounge the price of a cup of tea. No one seemed to have any money. I shyly placed the twopence upon the table.

'Thanks, kiddo!'

He tapped my shoulder lightly. Once more I flushed as all eyes were turned on me, then I was forgotten again, as some 'lucky sod' who'd won a scholarship to Rome was congratulated in his absence.

Only Michael seemed formally dressed in his dark brown corduroy jacket, shirt and tie, fawn flannels and polished shoes. He also possessed a watch, and half-a-dozen pencils protruded from his top pocket. His broad hands with perfect, strong nails at the end of straight fingers had never had much use, although they looked strong and capable. He used them expressively, moulding the air as he grasped for emphasis. Thick, tight, curled black hair with just a flash of pure white above the shells of his exquisitely shaped ears. . . .

Suddenly his eyes widened as he gazed at me, smiling quizzically. I'd been staring at him.

'I must go!' I said in some panic, but once more he delayed me.

'Come, don't run off again.'

He held my arm.

I was alarmed at the strange quickening his touch had upon me and felt suddenly breathless as I ran outside.

I knew that he would soon follow.

'Are you always so shy of me? Do you always blush when anyone talks to you?' He looked at me half-seriously, half-amused. 'Would you like to see St Martin's?'

Initially protesting, but unable to resist his persuasion, I meekly allowed him to escort me.

The students bent over their canvases with great earnestness. I thought their work was atrocious, faintly appreciating only one or two pictures that nearly resembled the subject who stood woodenly still.

In another room we came across a group oddly spaced around a girl with red hair standing completely nude. I was flabbergasted. I tried to put on a blasé air, but Michael noticed my embarrassment, as the inevitable flush gave me away.

We left St Martin's and walked, or rather ambled, to the National Gallery. Here he did his best to instruct me in the various traditional schools of art. He spoke like a teacher, but with infinite patience. At first I listened most attentively, but after a while his comments seemed somewhat pretentious and my interest in his words dissipated, but his willingness and the gentleness of instruction warmed me to him. His undivided attention to my education gave me a feeling of worthiness.

When we left the building, I was surprised to see that it was already dusk. We took the bus. Michael squeezed my hand in parting as we alighted together, and I raced home.

Pops had been alarmed at my disappearance. I explained where I'd been but his manner was quiet, his expression anxious, even mournful. There was no hint of censure and, when he spoke, it was with his usual gentle politeness.

I retired early, but my mind milled over the day's events and for a while sleep evaded me. I thought of my new-found friend; wondered when I would develop a normal bosom; tussled with the mixed feelings I had over seeing a girl without her clothes. I hadn't know that ears could be so perfect. . . .

Next morning I was up very early to put the finishing touches to my work. That done, I sped down the stairs and found Michael waiting in the hallway. He had dropped by for a chance of seeing me before he went into St Martin's. I was thrilled and surprised to see him, but wondered that he hadn't rung the bell.

The late autumn sun shone warmly for so early in the day as we walked over to the Swiss. There was no name over the front of the café. The continental owners, brother and sister, middle-aged and stockily built, rarely showed any expression except perhaps a slight pursing of the lips when someone lingered past an hour over a single cup of tea.

As we sat down, a rush of students immediately descended upon us, claiming his attention with their noisy greetings. Michael was swept away with them to St Martin's and I was left with just a wave from the door. For a time I sat there stirring my tea, now turned cold, and watching new arrivals who differed from the students, mainly workmen and a few interesting looking lay-abouts.

Then, reluctantly, I left to deliver my work.

Often, although not in any hurry, I would run, feeling the pleasure in movement. On one such occasion, I felt a warm hand grasp me. Again I felt the thrill of his touch and smiled back at him with a mixture of joy and confusion.

'You're not going to blush again?'

'I've been running,' I stammered, getting a deeper shade of red.

'Where are you off to?'

'Just shopping.'

'I'll come with you.'

He walked slowly with long strides, 'Don't you ever wear a dress?'

'I don't have any!'

'Doesn't your father buy you any clothes?'

'I don't seem to need dresses,' I said doubtfully, ashamed of my ill-fitting attire.

'You'd look pretty in a dress.'

I determined to acquire one in the immediate future, but now I felt naked and small under his scrutiny.

'Blushing again?'

'I . . . I just can't help it!'

'I'll cure you.' He took my shopping from me. Then, as we reached the bottom of the stairs leading to the flats: 'Can you come out tonight?'

'I've never been out in the evening without my dad.' His expression was quizzical. 'But I'm sure I can. Wait. I'll just go up.' I left him and ran up the stairs.

Pops was mending a tenant's window. Diffidently I told him that I'd be joining my friends that evening. His expression showed disapproval, but he mumbled that it was up to me. I suggested that I bring Michael up to meet him and, without waiting for a reply, I shot down the stairs, returning with a reluctant Michael.

Disappointed, I saw they seemed to take an instant dislike to each other, or rather the dislike was on the side of Pops, giving Michael an unpleasant feeling of censure. It was an awkward meeting, and I sadly realised that Michael would not care to expose himself to repeated visits.

That evening Michael took me to a chess club in Soho. In

one room chess was being played by an older generation of continental men. They sat intently watching the boards in front of them, a strange, shabby lot. We moved into an inner room where Michael asked if I was hungry. I said I hadn't eaten, whereupon he delved into his pockets, only to find his financial resources exceedingly low.

Pretending not to notice, I volunteered: 'I'm really not very hungry. Please, you eat.'

He silenced me by raising his hand, and, with yet another expansive gesture, summoning the waiter.

'Spaghetti Bolognaise, and please bring the cheese,' he commanded with an arrogant air, but added, smiling roguishly, 'For one only, but with two sets of cutlery.'

So we ate this unaccustomed dish, sitting on either side of the table, dipping into the same plate. I watched him with some fascination as he manipulated the long strands and he chuckled as I sought vainly to imitate his expertise.

Michael was frequently hailed and often wandered off as the club became more crowded later in the evening, yet he kept his eye on me. When occasionally some tipsy character would lurch over to me with a 'What have we here...?' Michael would come to my rescue.

My sharp ears picked up many conversations. So many ideas were thrown up by those who took the seats next to me. I never contributed to these discussions but listened intently, wondering at the things I'd never thought of, realising how I'd been blithely unaware of so much.

Someone called out the time. I was horrified to find it so late and sought out Michael. He offered to take me home, but remembering his slow stroll, I refused and ran home to find it past one o'clock.

Pops had waited up. He looked anxious and tired, but insisted on making me a cup of cocoa. While we sipped the boiling liquid, he suddenly became cheerful and talked of our plans for India. But I wasn't listening . . . I couldn't tell Pops that I no longer wished to go. I evaded the issue by yawning and insisting that I was about to fall asleep.

I was now going to the club almost every evening. As I became a little less self-conscious, I wanted to see more and more of this crowd, although I still felt very much an outsider. I was not an artist, a writer, a poet, a renegade or even a glorified vagrant; I had little to justify my intrusion into this society.

One night, I came home very late to find Pops had gone to bed. Propped up on the table I found a note:

> Dear Marian,
> I knew a fairhaired little child,
> Dainty, pretty, thoroughly wild,
> Grey-blue eyes and saintly face
> Endearing smile and elfin grace.
> We came to town, she loved to roam,
> Through the streets around her home.
> There she found strange new places,
> Bearded men with pleasant faces.
> Girls with charm, some were sad,
> Others gay and many bad.
> That fairy charm may die or fade
> As sunkissed head into the shade
> Of café, club and back street wanders,
> And to the whims of Soho panders.
> Must that sweet and lovely smile
> Fade away and turn to guile?
> > Love from
> > Pops x x x

This was more powerful than any rebuke. I'd not been unaware of my selfishness at leaving him alone. On the rare occasions that we had talked, I'd noticed sadly that he listened to my descriptions of my friends and new-found ideas in strained silence, and I had begun to think that he was not so fond of me any more.

That night I lay in my bed thinking of the time we'd been thrown together. How lucky it had been for me! Dear sweet Pops! Despite all the stealing and all the bad things I'd done, he'd never stopped loving me. But how to tell him that I just had to be with these people? That I found them exciting, that I had become aware of my appalling ignorance? Michael? I hardly dared to mention his name to Pops. How could I tell him that he filled my thoughts every day, that I longed only to be near him, to feel the touch of his hand?

One thing I was sure about. I had to educate myself. To think that I had thought that 'politics' was another Italian dish! I had nearly died with embarrassment. Too late to go to school . . .

I made up my mind I would read one hundred books.

SEVENTEEN

Confusion

The following morning, I found myself at the book shop.

Isolated subjects, presupposing some knowledge, stared down at me. For a while I felt defeat. Then I came upon the Pelican series, small slim volumes that held information on many subjects. After some deliberation I chose Sir James Jeans's *Mysterious Universe*. It had a powerful impact upon my imagination. I had felt insignificant before, and now this book made me believe it. The whole history of Earth, its eventual fading, perhaps its catastrophic disappearance, were but a fleeting spark in universal time. The ideas the book invoked were shattering, yet there was a magnificence and an extension of the precise order I had already grasped in earthly seasons, in a grain of wheat, in the seemingly heartless efficiency of ants. In the realisation that nothing disappears, only changes.

After two days of exploring the dizzy heights of the universe, I wandered back to earth. Pops had been pleased to see so much of me as I lay around with my book.

From time to time I still stored artifacts for my childish 'palace'. I included in it Pops's poem and the first of my 'one hundred books'.

The following day I set out in search of Michael, and found him with his friends fawning over a new arrival at the art school, his form leaning at an angle against the wall, his arm hanging loosely round the back of the girl's chair. After a moment's hesitation, I slipped into a vacant seat at the next table where at first I ignored the conversation until I realised that they were discussing the young woman whose unexpected presence had caused me dismay.

It seemed that she was a refugee from Hungary. She had let it be known that she was heir to a fortune of some twenty thousand pounds, to be hers at the age of twenty-five or upon her marriage.

Although I had quickly caught his eye on entering the café, Michael seemed hardly to notice my presence, and gave me only a slight nod by way of a greeting.

Michael often raised his voice unnecessarily to give his words emphasis. He was now promising to take her to the club this very evening and generally to put his life at her disposal in his offer to show her the sights of London.

The first pangs of acrid jealousy, consciously experienced, overwhelmed me. I had so longed to see him and to put my hand in his. . . . Unable to sit any longer, I rose from the table, but Michael was at the door before me. He gently grasped my upper arm and guided me outside where we stood for a moment.

'I've been asked to look after that poor kid until she settles down at St Martin's,' he confided almost apologetically.

'She doesn't look very poor to me,' I blurted out, not liking the sound of my own voice.

'She lost her family in the concentration camps.'

A sudden stab of guilt startled me. 'Oh please . . . I'm so sorry. Of course you must take care of her.'

My next book, *Man, Microbe and Malady* by Dr John Drew, so exquisitely but simply written, took me to another realm yet seemed to maintain that sense of supreme order and interdependency of all things. I spent many hours in lazy contemplation and wonder.

I heard that Michael was seen with his new friend in all our favourite haunts. I avoided him and hid myself with books. I gave up working with raffia, for when my brain was idle I would trace, with futility, the chaos of my feelings. In the Pelican series, I found books which brought stunning new horizons that took me completely away from nagging longings and the ache for a touch of a hand.

After a week of avid exploration amongst fragments of knowledge, I once more set off in search of Michael and found him in the café, unexpectedly alone. His face lit up.

'Where have you been?' he called to me as I joined a small queue at the counter.

He brushed aside crumbs with the edge of his saucer while pointing to the seat opposite. 'Have you been ill? You look pale.'

He sounded so concerned and immediately put out his hand. But I shrank from it, pretending not to notice.

'I've been busy,' I said casually, clasping my cup with both hands. 'Where is your lady love?'

'Oh her? I don't know. She's not particularly special. I like her and I have been thinking about her.' His voice was plaintive.

'Thinking about her?' I echoed.

'You cannot imagine what my parents are like. They want me to settle down, even get married!' He shuddered. 'I'm Jewish you know.'

He gave me an odd enquiring glance, but his words meant little to me. I thought of Jews as a nomadic tribe somewhat like gypsies, only educated.

'My parents are very orthodox, they drive me crazy sometimes. You cannot imagine . . . my life at home is so different. I'm the black sheep of the family.'

'What is orthodox?'

'Very religious. They're very strict, that's why you never see me around Friday nights. The Jewish sabbath starts on the Friday evening when the sun goes down and ends Saturday evening when the first three stars appear in the sky.'

I imagined his parents in the ritual of seeking the three stars. The idea struck me as romantic and paganistic.

'What if it's cloudy?'

Michael laughed. 'Oh the time's in the *Jewish Chronicle*, you silly.'

'Were you thinking of marrying that Hungarian girl?'

'Well, I did think of it. She's Jewish and rich, but no, I couldn't.'

'Couldn't you marry a non-Jewish girl even if you loved her?' I tried to sound matter-of-fact.

'Oh *no*! It would kill the old man. Besides, what would I live on? My parents would totally reject me. I couldn't live in poverty. I couldn't make money with my art, although I'll qualify as an art teacher, but I couldn't live a decent life on the money.' I'd never seen him so gloomy. 'I don't want to get married at all. If I did, well, it would have to be to someone with money.'

'Couldn't you get a job?'

'I could go into the family business. Both my brothers went in when they were fourteen. My parents want me to, but I can't visualise it. I'm not cut out for that kind of life.'

'What is the business?'

'Persian carpets. They're importers–exporters. Pappa goes to Persia buying and my elder brother helps him here, where they sell them to the better stores. I'm afraid we all fight like cat and dog, although we're really very close. I can't bear to think of working with my brothers, we really don't get on.'

'Can't you make your own life?'

He shook his head.

'Why not? And hell! You should be able to marry who you like!' I now felt a little anger on his behalf.

'Well, they were talking only last week of bringing a girl over from Persia for me. Can you imagine that? Sometimes I think my parents still live in the dark ages. My elder brother is married to our first cousin, an arranged marriage. I think they're happy enough, though.'

'Why don't you leave home?'

'I did, just over a year ago. I took a room in Swiss Cottage and nearly starved. I got pneumonia and had to go home.'

He went on describing that short experience with nostalgia and pride in the poverty he'd suffered. It was an experience he looked back to rather romantically. I smiled a little.

'Are you laughing at me?' He sounded cross.

'No, of course not!' Then I carried on, 'What then will you do when you leave St Martin's?'

'I thought of commercial art, but really, I don't want to join the rat race. That's more a prostitution of art.'

Baffled, not understanding his terms, I pressed him, 'You must have some idea of what you'll do later?'

'I expect I'll eventually land up in the family business, but I'll study art as long as I can.'

It seemed strange to me that religious people were in business at all.

'Does your mother work too?'

'Good heavens, no!' He laughed. 'We don't have women in business. It's unheard of in our community.'

Why ever not? I thought, but he went back to discussing his art.

'My teacher noticed I was good at drawing, said I should take it up. My mother despises artists, yet she's very pleased to show off my work.' He sighed. 'Sometimes I think of going off to South America. A gang of students are thinking of it. We'd live in a sort of settlement, like the people in Palestine.'

He suddenly became alive again and talked enthusiastically

of how they'd live in the sun, building their own huts, working the land and painting.

The spirit of adventure rose within me. 'Can I come too?'

'What about your dad? Anyway what can you do?'

I resented his implication. 'I can do anything. And my dad? He'd be very useful, he could come too.' I spoke with conviction.

'We'd all be artists. All men. Women would get in the way.' The arrogance of this statement I found stupefying. But he carried on. 'I don't suppose I'd go anyway. I have my parents to think of.'

'Your parents have other sons.'

'Ah yes, but our family, well, we all stick together.' Then abruptly he changed the subject. 'What are you doing over Christmas?'

'Nothing.'

'Would you like to come to a party?'

'Oh yes, I'd love to,' I cried with delight. 'I've never been to one.'

'You know, you're a sweet kid! I can talk to you . . . I feel you understand,' he said slowly, melting me with his smile.

Then he clasped my hand in his, and I felt the shock of his touch once more.

I'd been ready at six, although Michael wasn't to pick me up for the party until eight. I felt very self-conscious in the ill-fitting dress, which bagged where my bosom should have been. But my hair was brushed until it shone and the thought of being in his arms made my head reel. Then it occurred to me that I didn't know how to dance. Now I felt panic rising.

Pops eyed me anxiously.

'Don't be home too late, will you, pet? You look a little pale . . . and, oh, here's money for a taxi in case you want to leave early.'

201

Nine o'clock came and went, ten, eleven. He was not going to come! The let-down was devastating on top of the feeling that I looked ridiculous in the awful dress and the pretence to Pops that it didn't matter. I flung myself into bed and snivelled into oblivion.

I heard nothing from Michael and determined to avoid him in the future. Yet on the first day of term I found myself looking out of the window hoping to see him. He was not among the mass of those exchanging greetings around the entrance of St Martin's and I decided to tidy up the kitchen. This accomplished, I returned to the sitting-room and idly glanced out of the window again. My heart leapt as I saw him on the opposite pavement looking up at me. I parted the curtain, putting myself in view, and he beckoned to me.

Without another thought I ran down the stairs and dashed over the road unaware of the traffic until I heard the screeching of brakes.

'You crazy kid! You could have got killed!'

'You were supposed to have taken me to a party!'

'I should have phoned. My mother was ill and she listens in on calls. She'd want to know all about you. It was too difficult.' He spread his hands in apology.

I forgave him instantly.

'It's so nice to see you,' he said smiling down at me, dissolving any creeping doubts I had harboured.

Instantly heady happiness returned.

'Shouldn't you be in school?'

'I love the way you call Art College "school"! You don't think much of it, do you?' But he didn't wait for a reply, adding, 'I think I'll skip school.'

He had taken my arm and was guiding me along the pavement. 'I've got my brother's car today. How about going to Southend?'

'Oh, I'd love to, I'll go and tell my dad.' Exhilarated I darted across the road.

Pops thought we were mad. It was the beginning of January. I left singing: 'Oh I do like to be beside the seaside . . .'

Michael drove at breakneck speed and I felt not the least bit nervous, even when at one point we nearly went out of control on only two wheels around a roundabout.

Deserted mudflats stretched to the edge of the sea. Michael held my hand, like holding the hand of a child. We walked slowly, and at first in silence. I noticed little holes in the mud and longed to investigate, but could not let go of the joy of my hand inside his.

Then the chill quickened his pace and he began to tell me about his family and his earlier life.

His mother had been a mere child of thirteen, his father a stranger to her when they had married in the port of Alexandria, Egypt, before the First World War.

His father had begun his business by carrying a mountain of rugs upon his back and following behind the camel train. He had received a measure of protection from the wealthier merchants by acting as their servant at every halt of the caravan from Persia to Egypt. The journey across the deserts, following the old silk roads, had taken almost a year. Eventually he established a small business in Alexandria. Further expansion and prosperity enabled him to move with his family to Vienna at a time of political unrest and fears for the safety of the Jewish people.

Michael spoke of his father with pride and yet I knew that he feared him.

'Are you listening? Am I boring you?'

'Gosh no! What a family. I was just trying to visualise that journey. Your father must be immensely strong?'

'As strong as a bull!'

He told how life had been good to them until the rise of

Hitler. Then they had suffered many humiliations and his elder brother had been savagely beaten by Hitler Youth thugs. Intolerable conditions made them stay away from school. The family left for England in 1936. Arriving with virtually nothing, they shared a large house in Stamford Hill with other families fleeing from Nazi degradation.

Within a short time, his father owned the house and re-established his business. Now they were comparatively wealthy.

His family intrigued me. His parents, without books or schooling, had been able to survive great misfortune and hardship, indeed had built upon them admirably, giving this agreeable son of theirs innocent airs of material advantage.

We bought a fish-and-chip lunch, blowing on the too hot chips, playfully feeding each other while finding a little bowlegged man and his huge bow-legged lady immensely funny as they waddled ahead of us at a great speed.

Icy winds drove us away from the exposed sea front and we wandered around the deserted streets. The afternoon disappeared rapidly.

Painfully aware of him on the way home, I shyly asked him to kiss me when he deposited me in the hallway of the flats. His expression was surprised amusement, but he promptly kissed me on my forehead. I was shattered. Indignant and embarrassed, I wanted to run from him, but he held my arm, so I hid my face from him.

'Don't be upset. You can't go around asking men to kiss you,' he said gently, but I had now burst into tears. 'Come let's walk for a bit. Your father will wonder what's happened if you go up like this.'

We walked until we came to a churchyard and sat on a seat under a lamp. He put his arm round me as I shivered with the cold. Then he took out his handkerchief and demanded that I blow my nose. I was hesitant to soil his beautifully folded linen that shone so whitely but, not possessing my own, I did as I was bid.

'I'm not a child. I don't go around asking anybody to kiss me,' I suddenly cried angrily. 'I think I'm in love with you.' There! I had blurted it out! 'I'm sorry, I didn't mean to say that.' Sobbing, I felt utterly confused.

Michael looked stunned.

'You mustn't think of me like that. Nothing could ever come of it, can't you see that? I hadn't thought of you in that way. To me, you're my little friend. You're sweet and honest. Not like the girls I mix with.'

'But I'm not honest!' I cried, seeking somehow to qualify, 'I steal things, I always have!'

'What sort of things?'

'Books. I don't steal so much now but . . .' For a moment I was going to tell him my true background, but I checked myself, feeling that perhaps I had already gone down in his estimation.

'Oh, lots of people steal books. I've stolen a couple of things in my life, I guess.' Then he sighed. 'I think perhaps we should not see each other again. You're very young, you don't know what you'd be letting yourself in for. You mustn't think of falling in love with me.' He spoke sadly, then he took my head in his hands and tilted it up towards the light.

'Come on, no more tears, eh?'

'Only if you can forget what I said and I can go on being your little friend?' I smiled as I stood up, freeing my head as I did so.

'OK.' He rose also.

For a moment he stood looking at me, then took both my hands and pressed them to his lips. It was a gentle action, but it set my heart pounding. I snatched my hands away, but in a moment his arms were round me, his gentleness turning to passion. I was engulfed by the hugeness of his frame. He held me hard against his body as we kissed. I felt almost suffocated.

Then he let me go. I was trembling, dizzy from the fierceness of my own emotions.

'Oh God! I didn't mean to do that.' He almost sobbed and, turning away from me, sat down on the bench with his head in his hands.

I stroked his head. 'Please, I've wanted you to kiss me like that for ages.'

He looked up at me. 'I very nearly did more than that.'

Smiling mischievously, I whispered, 'I wish you had.'

'You confuse me. I thought you hadn't been kissed before?!' His eyes searched mine.

'I haven't.'

'Then you must be a natural.'

'What do you mean?'

'Never mind. I'm taking you home in case I get into trouble.' He was smiling again. We walked faster than his usual pace and, with obvious relief, he once more deposited me in the hallway.

'Kiss me again?' I asked cheerfully.

'Not bloody likely! I'll see you tomorrow, you wicked wench.'

Deliriously happy, I jumped into bed.

Forgetting school, work and even books, we spent weeks in each other's company haunting art galleries and museums. Sometimes, hand in hand in Oxford Street, Michael would gaze at men's clothes and shoes while I patiently waited at his side trying to fathom his enthusiasm over the same drabness of every display. I would also study the variety of brickwork and architecture above the shops. Seeking to influence my appearance, he would guide me to windows of young women's fashions, but I could not associate myself with the snooty-looking mannequins nor the frocks they modelled. I knew that my clothes were ill-fitting and past their prime, but the longer I attached a garment to myself, the greater my regard for it.

Indeed, I almost wept over my shoes when they finally fell apart.

In moments of rare privacy, we kissed luxuriantly. We were one of the couples raising heat in the back row of the cinema, or melting the latticework of frost on the windows in cavernous shop doorways after dark.

Michael chided me over my unkempt long hair which fell across my face in wisps. I noticed that his eyes made constant comparisons with girls in the passing crowd and resolved to visit a hairdresser. I telephoned for an appointment at a then famous salon.

In the unfamiliar surroundings I tried to assume an air of dignity. The fellow with the teasy-weasy, fringed hair-do held my long hair almost at arm's length while gently combing out the strands. Mumbling that it had been allowed to lose its strength, he proceeded to cut it within an inch of my head, laying the lengths carefully and appreciatively over the back of a chair.

He passed me a large mirror. My reflection caused me to gasp in horror. I looked like a convict. I thought of Michael and burst into tears. Disconcerted, the man flapped around and offered a free wash and set. My hair was crimped into a freakish bubble-effect. I left with a feeling of deep resentment. The hairdresser, I felt sure, had stolen my hair. The beast had preserved it so carefully.

'My God! What have you done?' Pops gasped.

Michael greeted me later with: 'Christ! You look even more like a boy. I shall be accused of being a queer.'

Then he refused to talk about future plans, dismissing me with: 'I must get back to my art. I don't want to be chucked out. My parents won't support me if I don't carry on.'

In utter misery I crept home to find consolation in books and in my ambition towards enlightenment. We saw less and less of each other. It appeared that Michael had forgotten me.

Now, as April brought my seventeenth birthday, I was designing and fashioning lampshades and selling them to Harrods. They took over three months to pay and by the time the money arrived I was working as a waitress and hating it.

EIGHTEEN

Fury

It was Friday evening, Michael was in the bosom of his family, and, in a belated celebration of my seventeenth birthday, Pops and I were walking out of Phoenix House. Arm in arm and in a happy mood, we were suddenly confronted by a woman with a shock of white hair.

She grabbed at Pops.

'Got you!' she cried explosively and glared at him with possessive triumph.

Then she thrust her wild eyes within inches of mine.

'Caught you in the act!'

Dear Pops's face blanched.

'Mummy!' I gasped disbelievingly as her image engulfed my senses.

Pops tried to evade her, but she had hold of his lapel. With her other hand she struck me a savage blow across my face.

'Harlot!' she yelled.

Letting go of Pops and snarling like a wild animal, she made, with her hands outstretched, as if to tear me to pieces. I turned, but my short hair was grabbed from behind and I was swung jerkily about with tremendous strength. Then she put her face, glowering, demented, close to mine.

'*Mummmeee. . . . Don't!*' I screamed.

There was an expression of puzzlement, then she let go.

Perhaps it was my look of terror that my mother recognised.

Very slowly she relaxed and moved back. I watched a tuft of my hair scurry about the floor of the lobby in the draught.

'Marian? Is it Marian?'

I nodded breathlessly.

'Oh, my baby!' She tried to put her arms round me but I pushed her off.

Pops and I exchanged glances. There was no need for words. We led her upstairs to the flat.

Still trembling, I made tea, while my brain worked frantically on devising some escape from her. Entering the sitting-room with a tray, I saw Pops turning out his pockets. His money she tucked into her coat and then she became intensely curious about his other bits and pieces. She pounced upon his keys, wanting to know what each one opened. I knew they were the pass keys for the tenants' flats, but Pops lied, saying that he'd found them and had planned to drop them into the police station. She pocketed them too.

She stood for a moment as if she were trying to remember something. My mind went numb as I watched her in fearful anticipation. Then began a fury of activity. She turned out the contents of drawers, angrily throwing everything upon the floor and asking us where we obtained this and that. She marched into bedrooms, creating the same havoc, and into the kitchen where she emptied the cupboards, flinging glassware, spilling sugar, lentils, soapflakes into a heap.

We both just stood and watched until her energy dissipated and she plonked herself breathlessly on a chair.

But it was only for a moment, for, from this position, she spied the cupboard above Pops's head. In a moment she had dragged the kitchen table and mounted it with the agility of a cat. I had thought the cupboards were empty; they were high up and we'd never used them. But she found some boxes and passed them to me.

'Get me down, George! Come on, worm, don't just stand there,' she cried.

Pops hovered about in a state of extreme anxiety. He moved like an automaton, and I watched him help her. She opened the boxes and laughed with a crazy exultancy.

She banged Pops about the head with one of the boxes and little packets of Durex contraceptives flew about the room. (I had no idea of the use of these unfamiliar items.)

She then began to accuse us of all sorts of obscenities, thrusting handfuls of condoms on the table to bear witness, she said, to our wickedness.

Suddenly she was tired. She got up and moved to the sitting-room where she sat restlessly drumming the table next to her. Refusing tea, she questioned us closely about her belongings. She said she was cured and was home for good.

The rest of the evening we spent in virtual silence. We watched her warily while she dozed, only to wake immediately should either of us stir. Eventually she agreed to go to bed, but insisted upon sleeping in my room demanding that Pops stay with her.

I sat on the floor outside my room, fearing that something dreadful would happen to Pops. I was ready to save his life if need be. I now realised that Pops had become a very precious anchor in my life.

Misery overwhelmed me. I didn't think of this threat as 'Mummy'. Somewhere, deep inside me, had I not signed 'Mummy' away and buried her? I started to feel crazy myself.

After some hours I rose, stiff and cold, from the floor. I crept quietly to the kitchen and made myself some tea, skirting the splattered heaps on the floor, and drawing a chair up to the shifted table. I realised that we must get rid of this terrifying, violent intrusion which obliterated rationality. I spent the rest of the night frantically scheming.

My world had crashed. Both Pops and I were in a state of

terror. Our fear was probably unreasonable, perhaps because neither of us ever mentioned my mother. I thought of her only in nightmares, and the immediacy of her violence at her reappearance shattered my senses.

The day was spent in strained watchfulness. I was grateful for the mess my mother had created in our previously immaculate flat as I busied about the tidying. Pops was not allowed out of her sight.

I made a late lunch which my mother tucked into ravenously. Then she fell asleep in the chair in the sitting-room.

I tiptoed into the kitchen, beckoning Pops to follow me.

We made our plans. Somehow Pops was to persuade my mother that they'd have an evening out, just the two of them, to celebrate her return. Then, when they had left, I would pack, leave the flat and find a room somewhere. I arranged to meet Pops in the A.B.C. café in Victoria.

Suddenly I became aware of my mother in the doorway and I raised my voice, pretending to have been discussing something else.

My mother looked up at the cupboard that had held the contraceptives. 'Where are they? Where are they?' she screamed.

As she renewed her evil accusations and demanded to take me to a hospital to be examined, she moved towards me, her whole body threatening me, her hands reaching out for a hold. I sprang at her, striking her with my fist with all my might. She fell. Immediately, a great blackening lump appeared at the side of her jaw. I stared at her, aghast at the results of my unforgivable action.

Pops helped her into a chair where she sat, subdued, for a long time just looking at me wonderingly, but saying nothing.

Then: 'Take me home, George,' she said suddenly, softly breaking the tense silence.

Pops called a taxi. She went, docile and bewildered. But no

sooner had they got down the stairs than I heard stamping and yelling.

She came up the stairs bellowing.

'That woman! That woman attacked me!'

I rushed into the kitchen. When my mother appeared, I was standing behind the kitchen table with a knife in my hand thrust out in front of me.

The taxi-driver came and went.

My mother stopped in her tracks and just stared uncomprehendingly at me.

Pops took her gently by the arm suggesting that he bathe her face. She followed him like a lamb. I held on to the knife, and in an instant of dreadful despair and self-disgust thought to use it on myself. Then the two of them were at the door.

'My husband is taking me out,' she announced imperiously.

After watching them go downstairs, I fell into a fever of packing. Then it occurred to me that I had no money, not a penny. In a panic I rushed out of the flat and crashed into one of the tenants. He caught me, laughingly, and then saw my distressed condition.

'Why, whatever's the matter, kiddo?' he said with concern.

This time my wits didn't fail me. 'My dad's had an accident in Brighton! I must get there, but I haven't any money!' I searched his face.

He quickly thrust his hand in his pocket and pulled out a wad of notes.

'A fiver do?'

I was stunned by so much and hesitated.

'Look, your old man can pay me back later.' He pushed the notes into my hand. 'Come on, kiddo! You get a train from Victoria. Can you manage?'

'Yes, thank you. Oh *thank* you!'

I couldn't believe my good fortune. Finishing the packing, I called for a taxi for Victoria Station.

I dumped the bags at the left-luggage office and then did the rounds of the shop window advertisements, eventually finding a room off Paddington Green. It was a small dark back room containing two single beds, a tatty chest of drawers and a curtained cavity in the wall for hanging space. The rent was thirty shillings. I paid two weeks in advance and left for the A.B.C. café.

Pops was already waiting outside, but I didn't notice him until he tapped me on the shoulder. I jumped out of my skin.

We picked up our luggage and arrived exhausted at our new home with only one pound between us. Food would have to wait; the money had to be reserved for fares for the new job Pops had to find. We could never go back! She must never find us again!

Pops had aged ten years in thirty hours. I persuaded him to tell me how he managed to escape her clutches. He'd taken her to a restaurant, but she'd said she was tired and wanted to go back to the flat. He'd managed to convince her that she could rest in a cinema. They'd sat through the first film, which had been awful. The main feature was more exciting. He had waited for a tense moment in the plot, and had slipped out, saying he 'wouldn't be a moment'. Then he was running away, towards Victoria.

That night I crawled into bed with a sense of hopelessness. Again I had been guilty of the unforgivable. I was soiled by my own actions and I felt the seeds of insanity within me in the violence I had expressed. Visions of my mother returning to the flat while I was packing caused me to start up from a half-sleep, but finally dreamless oblivion claimed me.

The next day Pops telephoned the hospital in Epsom. My mother had arrived there in the small hours of the morning by taxi. The driver had not been paid.

NINETEEN

Hang-outs

Pops quickly became busy in another job but I stayed holed up in that dingy room desperately wondering who I was. Agonising memories of my childhood love for a crazy mother, our hand-to-mouth existence, my acts of stealing flooded into my senses. Eventually, and a little sadly, I forgave myself and resolved for the thousandth time to seek goodness. I flung my mind back into books and it wasn't long before I was singing again.

Now, suddenly, I missed Michael.

It was early in the afternoon, but I made my way, half-running, to the chess club in Soho. I found him sitting, quite on his own, reading a newspaper.

I stood for a moment quietly watching him. I observed how studiously graceful, how sternly handsome, how beautiful he was. Then I approached, startling him.

'Where have you been?' he cried.

He questioned me a little crossly about my disappearance from the flat above the Phoenix Theatre, but I distracted him by my surprise at seeing my new landlord at one of the tables. He was one of the older, weary-looking continentals who spent hours slouched short-sightedly and silently over chess games. He promised to teach me how to play.

So it was that one evening he knocked upon our door, bidding me to follow him to his room for a chess lesson and a good coffee. I tagged behind him as he turned without waiting for a reply and shuffled heavily and slowly down the stairs.

He set about making the coffee in a corner of the room which was even darker and dingier than the rest of the house. The walls were lined with dusty books on rickety overloaded bookcases. A high desk was littered with papers, on which stood a large yellowed photograph of a grand-looking family. It was an odd studio picture of a rather severe, unsmiling couple with four children against an extravagantly contrived, painted backdrop.

I enquired politely: 'Who are these people?'

'Are? Are *not*! My Georgie, my babies. Gas chambers. All gone.'

He hadn't even turned around.

I almost knocked the photograph over. It was as if I had touched a terrible open wound. This was a subject I still could not dwell on without terror! It was too enormous a madness. It brought incomprehensible, nameless, stifling fears.

'You had someone there, yes?' he asked gently in heavy guttural accents as he handed me a large cup of fragrant coffee.

'No. No. It's just that it does not seem believable. I can't think about it. . . .'

'Believe me, it happened. People should think about it, they should think about it every day, so's they don't forget it!' he said vehemently. 'But come, I'm to teach you the chess?'

So he taught me the game and told me much of his life. Of how he had owned a fine factory. Of the school his children had attended and how clever they'd been. He told me that the Nazis had, bit by bit, taken away the freedom of the German Jews. He had left his family to arrange to smuggle them into France. While he was away from them, his wife and four children had been snatched in the night, taken to a concentration camp, and had perished.

'And vot am I doing here?' he would ask time and time again, shaking his head.

Soon I had, a little sadly, to say goodbye to his dark rooms. Things were looking up and Pops and I found cheerful accommodation in Scala Street in Soho.

Now more sure of myself, I would wander freely around the Soho streets. I came across another café where I saw familiar faces and many new ones. It was another hang-out for drifters. Here there was a greater variety of characters, some of whom I got to know. I'd sit back and listen to their chatter, sometimes longing to join in, yet half-afraid I'd be approached. But the older people, some of whom seemed sadly resigned to their role on the fringes of society, were the ones I felt some freedom to converse with. I understood them better. Less sure of absolutes, less aggressive, they did not cling to fixed justifications or judgements, and I could identify with some of their thoughts and conclusions. They were more tolerant of my ignorance and would patiently explain ideas and events at great length.

Some of them would take it upon themselves to protect me from the fouler elements of Soho. A couple of cheerful young women, who often surfaced for breakfast in the early afternoon, caught my attention. I envied their ease of manner and was astonished when it was explained that I should not mix with them for they were prostitutes. So naive was I that I thought prostitution sounded like institution and had to be something respectable! These girls had started off as waifs. Provocatively pretty and generous by nature, instinctively suggestive, they had wandered into a profession which suited them well.

The strange mixture of humanity that was the café society was something I could not keep away from. It never occurred to me that I was part of the throng.

The students considered themselves the élite. Then came the prophets. These were the fortunates who were able to combine benign philosophy and interesting appearance with independent means. Most had a touch of genius which would never be recognised. There was also the criminal element, and occasionally I glimpsed guns and razor-scarred faces.

At the bottom there were the bums, those who had nothing to offer and nothing to give, always on the scrounge for a cup of tea, a meal or a bed. Some spent their lives in wasteful daydreams, clouded with pessimism. One or two spoke with acrid, bitter cynicism on every topic, spitting out caustic with a strange logic and putting everything and everyone on trial with an air of controlled civility that struck a frightening chord in the back of my mind. But most were gentler.

One fellow constantly quoted from Fitzgerald's *Omar Khayyám*. At the time I thought it was his own poetry. 'Why tomorrow I may myself be in yesterday's seven thousand years!' Always half-drunk, a fiftyish, gaunt, merry-eyed, shock-grey-maned dancing apparition, he delighted in the company of youngsters who adored his company. 'This', he would say, dipping into the ash tray with a delicate finger and making two neat piles upon the table, 'is you and this is me! Ashes, all right?' He'd lean back with a deliciously dramatic air and quote, ' "Into this world and why not knowing, like water willy-nilly flowing, and out of it like wind along the waste, willy-nilly blowing!" ' Then he would give a great puff, blowing the ash away and exploding into a fit of coughing. 'Where is you and where is me?' he would enquire, roaring with laughter, which would set him off on another fit of choking. He would leave the café at pub-opening times with, ' "Another and another cup to drown the memory of this impertinence!" '

There was an elderly Irish doctor who took me to the dog-races. He liked me to pick out the names of the dogs he would bet on. Somehow, they seemed to win. He explained that he could not offer me a rake-off. 'It would spoil the luck.' He was avaricious, fussy and tetchy and after only two excursions I avoided him. Occasionally he would catch sight of me and run up with his folded newspaper and a proffered pencil begging me to mark a few 'winners' for him.

'Shakespeare Mac', the sweetest fellow ever born, introduced me to a new world of expression with his spoutings. A short, squat busker of infinite gentleness and slightly timorous, he would become grandeur itself when transformed by the words of Shakespeare.

Once, on a bitterly cold night, I held the hat for him while he trembled with the passionate delivery of some great speech. People kept their hands thrust snugly in their pockets.

'Bleeding bloody Philistines!' he cursed through chattering teeth. 'No culture!' He counted the coppers in the hat and walked stiffly away.

'Are you all right, Mac?' I called.

'I'm OK, sunshine. It's my legs, they're frozen.'

I dragged him home and made him wait outside the flat while I made him a cup of cocoa and gave him a set of Pops's long woollen underwear and sent him off.

Pops pursed his lips when I had explained my generosity which he could ill afford.

I longed to talk to Pops about some of the ideas I found attractive, but he would listen with a sort of tolerance that I found irritating. I needed to communicate with someone who could debate and reason beyond my experience. Michael said that I was already too intense and that my ideas were just emotional. 'You should try to be normal,' he would cry, thus dismissing any hope of serious conversation.

It was then that I became a serious writer of quickly discarded, misspelt, peculiarly worded epistles.

'You're Persian Mike's girl, aren't you?' someone said.

The phrase thrilled my senses.

Michael had been concentrating on school while I took on casual work: hand-painting meter dials, waitressing, operating an addressograph machine with the sound of tin cymbals. Frequently my employers were unappreciative of my nimble abilities and paid very badly. Between jobs, the cafés beckoned me. Michael demanded that I didn't speak to the 'load of bums' who had become my friends. I ignored this instruction.

Christmas brought the usual round of parties which robbed me of Michael's company. Celebrations at the Art School; treasured invitations from professors; family acquaintances who used the air of festivity to reap an attendance from the prodigal son of the Persian community. So many! It was a surprise, therefore, when Michael asked me to an all-night do.

The party was given by the widow of Godfrey Phillips of some manufacturing fame who kept up a tradition that every Christmas poverty-stricken artists were to be fed. Michael bought me a dress in which I felt dreadfully ill at ease, but I consoled myself with the thought that he had chosen it himself.

We arrived late. Already a hard frost hung upon the hedge. Once inside, the warmth and the hubbub of music and conversation were overwhelming. Michael eagerly approached old friends and I just stood taking it all in.

An elderly lady took me by the hand and enquired who I was and in what field of art I strove. I told her that I was a poet. She begged me to recite something. Shyly I evaded her and accepted a proffered glass of wine, my first alcoholic drink since the cider in the flax field. I took another, for the first had been lightly delicious. Almost immediately my head span. Then I felt the clasp of Michael's warm hand upon my arm and I was being towed through the now crowded rooms towards the dance floor. He endeavoured to guide my nervous body, holding me alarmingly close, then he set me aside with evident disappointment and was soon dancing elegantly with one competent girl after another. A cry came from a sea of smiles. 'Mike, remember me?'

Finding it unbearable, I wandered off into other rooms seeking the remembered heat of the stifling kitchen, glimpsed in passing cluttered with interesting skeletal turkey and fish corpses. Now the food was being replenished and avid arms urgently sprang from the good-natured greedy throng. I watched in amazement as they tore the food apart with their fingers.

'Come to wallow in the height of decadence?' A young man laughingly offered me a turkey leg.

Then the group guffawed out, leaving a red-faced matron with pursed lips silently tidying up the mess. She pointed towards a pile of plates and I proceeded to arrange with some attempt at artistry a plate for Michael and another for myself while she looked on with a softening expression of approval.

For a while I could not find Michael. Then he was behind me grasping me possessively, nearly knocking the plates out of my hands. Chiding me for my absence for the best part of an hour, he seemed to think I was having too good a time without him. He could not have known that I had been miserable.

He instructed a fellow my own size to teach me the waltz and the quickstep. Under his watchful gaze we danced, but not with any real ease. I was trying too hard and my awareness of Michael's frowning observation sent me into a confusion.

It was now four in the morning. The dancing had long ceased and for an hour or so intense conversation about art erupted from the few not lying exhausted or drunk.

Our hostess, still alertly charming despite her seventy or so years, led us upstairs. She took it for granted that Michael and I were lovers, for she showed us to a single bed, pointing to another, just to be made out in the dim light, indicating with her finger to her lips that it was occupied.

We slipped silently into the bed, both clad chastely in our underwear. Michael said nothing.

'Kiss me goodnight,' I whispered.

But he drew away from me to the very edge of the bed. I lay accustoming my eyes to the reflection of the street lamps, unable to sleep, throbbing and aching with longing. I touched him shyly.

'Go to sleep!' he growled.

I had dreamed of this moment a million times and his rejection burned until I exploded into sobs. He turned and stroked my hair. I put my arms round him, coaxing and kissing him until he could resist no longer.

A dull winter and a cold wet spring seemed to disappear in an ecstasy of lovemaking. I was happy just to adore Michael. We would go for long, almost silent walks, often as far as the magnificently solid Battersea Power Station where we would look over the parapet to the river. His normally slow amble now seemed jaunty. We'd hold hands and laugh, and stop and kiss. I thought I would burst for the love of him.

Occasionally, we'd arrive at the club where he'd be greeted like a long-lost hero, patted and grasped by those eager for his company. I would find myself on the fringe, following with humble approval every graceful movement of his hands, every subtle change of his expression.

Pops was on night shift porterage in an exclusive hotel. I pretended not to notice his suspicion and disapproval. He had once caught us in bed together and had quietly left.

Suddenly the sun shone and the spell broke. Michael returned to his studies. A new occupation claimed him: the Oasis swimming pool. Determined to teach myself to swim, I would go to the pool early in the morning, slide into the loathsome cold and make rapid moves to the bottom. One morning in the changing room, I caught sight of myself in the full-length mirror for the first time. Blue around my mouth, my fine hair stuck to my head, and shaking from head to foot uncontrollably, with a slimy substance profusely dribbling from my nose. I felt suddenly panic stricken, aghast at my ugliness. Michael must never see me like this.

He swam like an eel while I watched dangling my feet over the edge, in envy of the girls with whom he played in the water. I was a little over six stone in weight. I would press my thighs on the edge of the seat to give them a certain roundness, and keep an open book before me to shield my lack of feminine charms as my swimsuit bagged in front of me like burst balloons.

It was the first summer I'd spent in London, and I grieved for the green fields of the countryside. It was hot and the streets were deserted, the cafés three-quarters empty, and even the wide boys and prostitutes seemed to be on holiday.

Michael spent days away. I never enquired where he had been. My demands were addressed to the air, often in the form of the latest songs sung softly, dramatically mournful, fit to break my heart.

For a while I had stopped my singing, feeling an inability to confront emotions. Michael sneered at shows of intense feeling. Yet it seemed to me that my emotions dictated my powers of perception.

I had lost a lot of my self-consciousness with other people but I was becoming more inhibited in communication with Michael. While I longed for him and eagerly awaited his company, his criticisms often left me with feelings of desperate inadequacy.

One day Pops informed me that my mother was dead. He said it quietly. I felt nothing, nothing at all, and was amazed that the news hadn't stabbed at my bowels. So intense about so much, perhaps I did not dare let out the demons of emotion. After a time I felt sadness and a sense of waste, but I couldn't dwell on the loss, not through pain, but because I couldn't find any answers and felt that there weren't any to be had. That was perhaps the chief hurt. Blind acceptance and the need to accept blindly.

So it seemed that I tossed aside and forgot, along with the denial of my beginnings, the life of my dearly loved mother.

TWENTY

Deliverance

A year was spent working at various jobs for short periods. Café society had begun to pall. I saw Michael less frequently and my fears that he had tired of me left me at a low ebb.

Suddenly the thought entered my head: *Mummy is dead! How? Where was she buried?* It was if I had to find a reason for my sense of grief and had at last directed my pain down an older avenue.

Early morning found me on a train to Surrey.

Visions of my mother. Sitting sometimes for days, so still, cross-legged like an Indian. Staring ahead with a far-seeing look in her eyes, while the only movement was the smoke from her cigarette in her upheld hand emphasising a certain mystical air that clung about her. Stains of blood on her sheets. The joy of laughter and sweet sayings. The knife she held above my head in the moonlight. My betrayal . . .

I wept uncontrollably for love of my mother. For regret. For the big black bruise on the side of her face. For myself. For my sins.

'Miss? Can I help?' A large man offered his handkerchief.

'I'm sorry.'

'Tell me about it,' another passenger demanded gently.

'My mother just died,' I said simply.

It was true. It had just hit me.

This area seemed the bleakest place in the world. I walked for miles and lost my way but arrived at the hospital in the late afternoon.

Enquiries at the desk proved unhelpful but persistence took me to a sympathetic young doctor sitting in a room at a desk with my mother's file in front of him. An urgent telephone call demanded his presence elsewhere and he begged me to wait for him. In a moment I had the file and was running out of the hospital.

In the days that followed I pored over the unfamiliar jargon. With the aid of the library, I came to an awful conclusion. My mother had died under an insulin-induced coma. I deduced that the doctors had experimented with putting her into 'deep sleep'. I had read that American film stars, demanding rest for their 'nerves', had been given insulin to quieten them down.

The realisation replaced grief with an awesome anger and an understanding of the impotence of those in Nazi concentration camps. Finally, and perhaps wisely, I burned the file that had poisoned my days and nights.

I sought refuge in my one hundred books. How people lived in the Middle Ages; the fundamentals of physics; the thrill of discoveries in archaeology; the structure of the earth; the basis of genetics. My study was haphazard and allowed long periods of gazing into the air in lazy contemplation.

Michael would toss my books aside. He said I was becoming a little odd. Nevertheless, I felt an almost wild excitement in discovery, and these paper platters were consumed with an urgency that took me out of myself and relieved the pain of waiting for him.

I stole a very large book, a present for Michael, but immediately regretted it. I'd had to walk past many idle assistants with exquisite fear rising within me, knowing that an observant eye could easily spot the ill-concealed bulk. As I left the shop I almost felt the touch upon my arm, but I had imagined it and was still free. It was then that I finally resolved that I must resist the awful temptation to steal because it threatened my liberty.

Some time later Michael told me that he had been given a number of watches to sell by ... well he didn't tell me except that his name rhymed with 'louse'. Positively not stolen, the watches had come 'through unusual channels', enabling them to be sold at less than half price.

Poor Michael, I found him very despondent. His first attempt in the business world was a dismal failure. He had not sold a single watch and the commission on each was a tempting ten shillings.

It seemed money for jam. Enthusiastically I volunteered to sell them for him. I hawked them around the cafés, but no one had any money, so I went further afield, remembering the large A.B.C. café near Victoria Station which always seemed so crowded.

Having got myself a cup of tea, I plucked up courage and joined a table where a company of workmen was sitting. They watched with amusement as I slowly laid a timepiece upon the table and offered it for sale.

'Let's have a look, duck,' one man said amiably.

I showed him the large flashy face with the extra fancy knobs. He handled the watch gently and with a certain wistfulness.

'Quite something, ain't it? What are you asking for it?'

'Four pounds?' I had meant it to be a statement.

He put it to his ear. 'Reckon it works?'

'My boyfriend bought it only last week. He paid eleven or maybe twelve pounds for it, but he can't afford to keep it after all and I said I'd try to sell it for him.'

He passed it round. They all admired it but none of them would buy it.

'Thursday's a bad day for flogging things, nobody has any

money on a Thursday. Try them blokes over there.' He pointed to three men at another table.

I picked up my cup of tea and hesitantly walked over to them and touched the back of a vacant chair. 'Mind if I join you?'

'Please do.' But it was said rather doubtfully.

This time I said that a friend had gone out of business through ill health and I was selling them off at a loss for a small commission. I showed them a number of watches. They carefully examined them and then coldly assured me that they had perfectly good watches of their own.

As inconspicuously as possible I carried on from table to table for the best part of an hour, getting a little bolder every time. People were surprisingly friendly and although I had not sold a single watch, I was enjoying myself tremendously.

Then, sitting by myself facing the exit some distance away, I saw three men enter the café. Almost instinctively I knew that they were policemen. They stood for a while looking around and then made straight for me. I suddenly felt like a frightened rabbit. They took an age to reach me.

'Good evening,' said the first man very politely.

'I understand you have some watches to sell?' queried the second.

'Oh, yes, I have!' My voice sounded strange. I tried to smile but my mouth felt tight and unreal.

'We are police officers. Would you mind coming to the police station? We would like to make a few enquiries.'

'Oh, I haven't done anything wrong, have I? The watches are not stolen!' I felt myself blanch and my legs were all atremble. I wanted to cry out for them to let me go home, but I just stood up.

'Come on, Miss,' said the first policeman in a kindly tone.

I followed them lamely to the car and was driven to the police station.

I racked my brains. What had Michael said? He said that

they had come from Switzerland by unusual channels. Well, I wouldn't say I'd got them from him, I'd dream up something. But I was stricken by fear and I couldn't think properly.

'Where did you get these?' The officer pointed to the watches now laid out upon the table.

'They are not stolen! Why did you bring me here?'

'Just answer the question.' He sounded almost bored.

'I met a man in the A.B.C. café. It was earlier on. He asked me to sell the watches for him, said he'd give me ten shillings for each one I sold.'

'This man, what did you say his name was?'

'He didn't tell me. I was supposed to be meeting him later tonight.' I sought vainly to improve the story. 'He did say he'd keep an eye on me so I couldn't run off with the watches.'

'I'm afraid I don't believe you. You'll make it a lot easier for yourself if you tell us the truth. We happen to know these watches. They've turned up all over the place. They're part of a consignment that has come to England without the custom duty being paid. This is a very serious matter. You know, it could involve a prison sentence of at least six months! So, come now, tell us the truth, and we'll probably let you go home.'

I knew now that I would have to stick to my story. I couldn't possibly have Michael sent to prison. Such a calamity for him was unbearable! The shame of his family was unthinkable!

'Listen, you're nineteen, and you've no business getting mixed up in this sort of thing. We'll find out in the end, you know. I've got a daughter of twenty and I wouldn't like her to see the inside of Holloway Prison.'

'I've told you the truth,' I said emphatically, but his words struck a chill in my soul.

'In that case, there's nothing I can do for you, is there?' He rose and opened the door for me most politely. 'However, if you should change your mind you can ask to see me.' He motioned to the waiting policewoman. 'Right, take her down!'

So I went down.

Down! Down! Prison for six months? Oh Michael, six months? What time is it? I mustn't think about it all. 'Boys and girls come out to play, the moon is shining bright as day. Leave your supper and leave . . .' So I sang in my head to block out the terrors of the immediate future.

The policewoman took me to another office where my fingerprints were taken. The man asked if I had had this done before and I shook my head in denial.

'So you've not been in trouble before?'

'No,' I whispered.

He sighed, shaking his head. 'We're trying to contact your father. We'll get him here as soon as possible. Perhaps he'll talk some sense into you. Want to tell me about your boyfriend?'

'I don't have a boyfriend,' I answered quickly.

Then I was taken to a cell and gently searched by the police-woman.

'Don't give me any bother. You'll have to stay here until we're told what to do with you. I've more than you to deal with. Keep your chin up, eh?' With that I was left alone.

The cell looked familiar. The same white tiles and the same lavatory the other end. Convulsive sobbing overwhelmed me. I took deep breaths to try to calm myself, but a wave of insane desperation clutched at me. I saw visions of corridors, stone corridors. Mops and iron buckets and horrid women with leer-ing grins and red chapped hands. By the time the cell door was opened some hours had passed and I was composed and resigned to whatever fate had in store for me.

The policewoman led me back to the office where Pops was now seated. He rose, his face ashen. I looked at him bleakly, beseeching his forgiveness. It hurt me terribly to see him like this.

The man at the desk turned to me. 'We searched your home and we found these.' He pointed to a small pile of watches on the table. 'I think, for your father's sake, you should tell us how you came by them.'

Pops's eyes met mine. Instinctively he knew of course where I had got them. I pleaded silently that he should disclose nothing.

'Do you think your daughter is shielding someone, sir?'

He looked closely first at Pops, then at me and back again to Pops.

'I'm sure I don't know.' Pops seemed immensely sad.

The man seated at the desk got up wearily and stood in front of me. 'Have you nothing else to add to your statement then?'

'I can't think of anything else I can say. But please, may I smoke? They've taken my cigarettes.'

He took a packet from his jacket and offered it to both of us. Then he left the room. A younger policeman remained but he was seated far away.

We started to talk in fast undertones.

'Please, Marian, tell them what they want to know. *Please*, for my sake! They're not letting you come home unless you change your story. I couldn't bear it if they took you away. Did Michael give them to you?'

Poor Pops, his big blue eyes looked so pained.

'Oh no! Michael knows nothing about them. Please say nothing about Michael. They may go to his home. Pops, I know the story seems unlikely, but it's true, really it is! What else can I say?'

I felt the tears of misery starting all over again.

'If it's that fellow, I'll never forgive him! I've not said it before, but he's no good to you and never will be.' Pops looked at the floor, his face colouring.

'Don't worry Pops. It'll be all right! And you don't know Michael. If you did, you wouldn't say such things.'

But Pops only sighed.

The policeman came back. 'I'm afraid, under the circumstances, we can't let your daughter go home. She will have to appear in court tomorrow.'

Pops stood up. 'I would see that she went to the court. I would stand surety for her.'

'I'm sorry, sir. You will see your daughter in the morning.' With that Pops was ushered towards the door.

'Bye, pet, take care.'

He tried to smile, then he was gone.

Dream-walking, I was led back to the cell and very soon taken to a waiting 'Black Maria'. Another young woman joined me and a slow trek around other London police stations, collecting other unfortunates, finally brought us to the gates of Holloway Prison. Fortunately it was dark so I couldn't then see the hideous structure.

Emotionally exhausted, I went through the ritual of inspection of belongings; a boiling, disinfecting bath; and a search for lice. I accepted my circumstances now with fatalistic calm.

My clothes were taken from me and I was pleased that the calico nightdress I was given was long-sleeved and warm. I wondered what my cell would be like, but I was taken to a door which, when unlocked, opened into a dormitory. It looked like a hospital ward. I was shown a neat bed which I immediately slipped into, not daring to glance around.

It was early in the evening and I lay on my side buried under the sheets, listening to soft chatter and occasional laughter. Later I was shaken to accept a welcome mug of cocoa. Looking around a little apprehensively, I was surprised to see that my company was representative of any group of women in any community.

The following morning, after a hurried but ample breakfast, I was driven in the police van to the court. I sat in silence for hours, smoking. Then a policewoman called out my name. I sprang up with relief, anxious to get the ordeal over.

'Sit down! You're not to get up unless you're told you may.'
Then she turned to a very tall woman. 'She's over there.'

The tall woman winced at the full impact of the police-woman's voice as she raucously bellowed: 'You boys, move along there and let the lady sit down!'

'Marian?'

Her look was searching.

I nodded.

'My name is Miss Hamilton. I'm a probation officer. I'm here to see if I can help you, but first we have to get a few things straight. I believe you said that this was the first time you had been in trouble?'

'Yes,' I replied guardedly.

'But it isn't, is it? You have quite a record, haven't you?' Her eyes sought mine.

I drew away from her, my head tilted up in a defiant gesture, but I said nothing.

'We're not going to get very far like this, are we?'

'I suppose not,' I replied bleakly.

'Let's see, you live with your father? Are you happy with him?'

'Oh *yes!* I'm very fond of him. He's very good to me.'

Miss Hamilton carried on her questioning for about fifteen minutes, all the time watching my face and reactions. Her manner was somewhat austere, yet she seemed sensitive.

Then I pictured her going over my record. That handbag! She would believe me capable of anything. She was thinking of that incident right now. Miss Hamilton was frowning, her eyes narrowed. Was she trying to imagine me in the act of assault? Loathing the remembrance, I was overcome with a sudden despair. How could she want to help me? Now my attitude became sullen and unresponsive.

'I'm going to ask for a fortnight's remand. I have to get to know you better.' She touched my shoulder, for my eyes were cast upon the floor. 'Do you want me to help you?'

'Yes,' I said without hope.

I couldn't work out what she meant by 'helping me'. How could she help me? The charge was *Being in charge of watches knowing they were uncustomed*, or something of that sort. An offence I had readily admitted to, naively reasoning that this must be only a minor misdemeanour, for, at first, I'd thought that they had suspected me of theft. So how could I not be convicted?

Miss Hamilton left and I put her out of my mind, dismissing her as one of those ineffectual, nosy-parkering do-gooders who are often found at the scenes of misery.

Then dear Pops came. He had an expression of false gaiety and presented me with a stack of cigarettes. 'Don't worry, pet. We've been in a mess before. We'll get over this one and start again when it's all over.'

But I could see the apprehension in him and I was sorrier for him than for myself.

Time dragged on, but finally at three o'clock in the afternoon I was called to enter the courtroom. Blood rushed to my face and my movements seemed difficult to control as I lurched awkwardly before the bench. Looking only at the Magistrate, I was aware of a sea of faces around me. A man stood up. I was conscious of the movement. He read out the charges in the sonorous voice of a preacher. Then it was quiet, except for a few coughs and the rustling of papers on the Magistrate's table. A policeman gave evidence of my arrest.

Then I heard the voice of a man introducing himself as a representative of the Customs and Excise. After calling on the court to be aware of the gravity of this crime, he started to spit out my previous convictions. His vitriolic tongue attacked my character, begging the court to make an example of me.

234

'Look at her! I have to tell you, she is no innocent offender! She has already been accused of violent assault and robbery!'

I turned to look at this man. He called me a menace to society. I found him frightening as he mouthed his words with evil eloquence.

'I object!' It was Miss Hamilton, the probation officer. 'I object to the picture drawn of this young woman.' Miss Hamilton sounded angry and fierce. 'I am aware that there are circumstances not mentioned in this court. I request a remand for this girl for a psychiatric report.'

In my fright I thought that I was going to be locked up because I was insane.

Miss Hamilton's voice was alive, pleading for me, but I hardly listened to the words.

'. . . She is living with her stepfather. Her own father committed suicide and her mother died in a mental hospital.'

'No! No! *No!*' I yelled, convulsed by hysterical sobs. 'That has nothing to do with it. Nothing to do with it.'

There was some consternation and I was led out by two policewomen.

'There, there!' said one of them, outside. 'You shouldn't have done that! Miss Hamilton's doing her best for you. You couldn't have been luckier, getting her.'

They begged me to try to compose myself, which I managed to do after drinking a glass of tepid water. I returned to the courtroom.

The Magistrate spoke. 'Are you feeling better? You may sit down if you wish.' I nodded, but gripped the rail in front of me.

'We have decided to remand you for a fortnight. You will do your best to be co-operative in order that we may see the best course to take with you. You understand?'

Outside the courtroom I had another interview with Miss Hamilton.

She smiled. 'Sorry if I upset you. That man ought to be shot! He gives me the shudders.'

Her manner was changed, and I warmed towards her.

She sat down on a bench next to me.

'May I ask you a question?'

'Yes.'

'Do you feel you can trust me? If I say that your answer will not be repeated to anyone if you so wish . . .?'

I knew the question she was going to ask, so I just nodded.

'Who gave you the watches?'

'I can't answer that.' I was almost sorry.

'Are you afraid of coming to some harm from the person who gave you them?'

'No, oh no!'

'Would you rather go to prison for six months than expose this person to possible prosecution?'

'Yes!' My answer was definite.

'All right. You are shielding someone then?'

'Yes.'

'Then we'll leave it at that. I shan't ask you again, but if at any time you'd like to tell me, you will, yes?'

She was as true as her word, for she never did ask that question again.

Transported back to Holloway Prison, this time in daylight, I was still unable to see its turreted drabness, for the windows of the van were blacked out. Again I had the disinfecting bath and search for infestations.

The first week passed with little occupation, some cleaning, but mostly spent reading uninspiring trivia. I was taken to be physically examined and then to the psychiatrist. She was a pleasant enough woman who asked if I found my lack of formal education a handicap. I said that I didn't think so. She said that I had been a fool but was possibly quite intelligent and I should try to put my obvious capabilities to some good use. She did not inform me of the substance or area of these capabilities, but I left her with a sense of some acknowledgement.

In the second week I was passed to a warder for questioning. She was almost a caricature, with a very masculine appearance. A few coarse hairs protruded from her chin; she had no neck and her manner was belligerent and insensitive. She threatened violence, using fairly obscene language. Perhaps there was some personal gain for her in obtaining information.

'Stand still, you runt!'

She walked round me and lifted up my blonde hair, sniffing. 'You stink!' I'd had a good scrub that very morning. 'V.D. that's it! I can smell it a mile away. Phew, you lot make me sick. We'll have a look at you.' She pressed a button and another warder arrived.

'Go on, up on the table.'

'No. I've seen the doctor!'

I felt a fear rising within me.

She leered at me. 'I said you bloody get on that table!'

I looked at the other warder, but her cowed, anxious eyes warned me to obey.

Roughly examined, I felt the sharp pain of what might have been a pencil. I was in some kind of a nightmare. When I was allowed to get down, I felt very angry at what had been a gross violation.

'You seem all right. You're lucky! But there's no telling what you can pick up in here. You know, you could even pick up V.D. Accidentally. Sometimes the swabs get mixed up. It's been known. It's a terrible thing, the whole of your insides get diseased!'

It didn't seem possible that this was happening to me. There was no escape. I stood my ground and looked directly ahead.

'Give me land, lots of land, la la la la la-la-la, don't fence me in . . .' The song saved me, although I couldn't remember the words.

The two interminable weeks came to an end and I was back in court and waiting on the familiar bench fully prepared for my six months' sentence. Astonishingly I received two years' probation, having to report to Miss Hamilton once a week for the duration of that time.

Poor Pops, he wept with relief and the two of us celebrated my freedom with an airing in the park, followed by a meal. That night I slipped into my bed, pushing aside the recent past with attention to J.W.N. Sullivan's *The Limitations of Science*.

I determined that I would never again do anything that would jeopardise my freedom. I would set about taking the good advice of Miss Hamilton, applying myself to agreeable, stable employment, and advancing my knowledge in all things, conscious that the more I learned, the less I knew.

Two further weeks passed, two weeks in which I tried to obliterate a gradual resentment which led to despair, before Michael appeared.

I had not heard his step upon the stairs. A light, mysterious, hesitant tap upon the door engaged my curiosity.

'Come in,' I called.

Michael walked into the room and over to the window. His head bowed, he stood with his hand to his forehead.

We were silent.

I watched tears splash upon the linoleum floor, and felt for a moment a detached amusement, deducing that the wet patches must be at least an inch across. When he turned round he was a picture of contrite misery.

'I had no idea! I would not have let you! I was not aware! I was so scared! My darling, I'm so sorry!'

I couldn't believe it. He had simply no notion, no understanding. I tried to tell him about my ordeal, but he shut me up with kisses.

'It's over! You mustn't ever mention it! We'll forget it, my darling!'

It felt very unsatisfactory. I wanted to point out that it was *not* all over, that I had to report once a week for two whole years, but he put his hand over my mouth.

'Hush! It *is* over!'

Picking me up, still covering my mouth, he took me to my bed where we proceeded to blot out the pain. The effect was only temporary. We never talked about it, and the hurt was buried in me.

'Cup of tea, my darling Pops?'

'It's a treat to see you smile, my pet.'

'Oh Pops, I really feel free. Free of so much.'

'What about Michael?' Pops said quietly.

'Oh, I don't know. Most of me will always be me.'

Then I got up from the table and started prancing around him, singing:

> 'It's a lovely day tomorrow,
> Tomorrow is a lovely day . . .'

followed by. . .

> 'Oh, oh, once again,
> My heart doth sing,
> A ring a ding ding . . .'

Pops chortled with delight.

'We'll make out, pet,' he said happily, after I'd finished clowning.

Epilogue

I am now a grandmother, but I still walk from the hip and can still thread a fine needle with my eyes closed.

By nature, I am fairly solitary, but I love people and can converse easily on a large range of subjects. My interests are innumerable, and I'm still learning. I try to stretch my mind, and stretching is perhaps all I do to keep fit, although I'm known to prance around a bit at times.

After a prolonged courtship, involving becoming Jewish, I eventually married Michael and became established in my 'palace', then disguised as a large, derelict, semi-detached house. We raised three lovely children, and we now have three delightful grandchildren.

By letting me be, Pops allowed me the privilege to sort myself out and relate to the real world. He remained at my side throughout the rest of his life, leaving me, and my palace, only when he was eighty-four.

More than thirty years ago Dorothy and I were reunited. She was married with two children and brilliantly speaking another language with apparent ease and fluency.

Still a powerful personality, she has a large capacity for

humour. She became a sought-after teacher, has now retired in idyllic circumstances on the borders of Switzerland, and is much respected in her community. Sadly, Dorothy lives far away from me.

After nearly fifty years, thanks to the Salvation Army, I found Millicent and Anthony both within the space of a week.

When she was informed of my whereabouts, Millicent telephoned me.

We were both so overcome with emotion that we could hardly speak, only weep – for all those lost years, for all that need we had of each other.

Between the howls we managed something.

'Oh God,' Millicent exclaimed, 'you sound so posh.'

'Oh no, I ain't. Really, I ain't,' I cried. 'It was all those years with Mother.'

'Oh God, she was *dreadful*.' A moment's hesitation then: 'What years?'

Of course we knew nothing of what had happened to each other. How could we?

Millicent has a husband and a son, and lives in a sweet little house not too far from London. But the loss of her family when she was a young girl meant a loss of support, a loss of identity, even a loss of self-esteem. We love her now. I want her to look in the mirror, smile at herself that lovely smile, and tell herself that she's wonderful, just because she damn well is.

She is funny when nudged into it. Like me, she has lost most of her good looks; but who needs these compensations of youth? She is still slim and straight, a little chesty as she apologetically lights another cigarette.

'This'll be the death of me,' she says.

And as I too light up: 'Gosh, you don't smoke, for heaven's sake?'

I giggle. 'I *burn*.'

'You're still wicked,' she laughs.

Anthony lives in the sunshine of southern Europe, but happened to be in England with his beloved daughter when he was contacted.

Confounded by the prospect of three sisters, three possible gold-diggers? – harridans? – so belatedly re-entering his life, he paused for thought – and fear – before bravely getting in touch with me.

I held court in my palace. I invited a couple of close friends and all the members of my tribe. Millicent, her husband and son arrived first. Anthony, his daughter, son-in-law and grandson soon followed.

After initial confusion as to who was who, it wasn't long before Anthony stole all the thunder. He sat grandly displaying a fine beard and wicked eyes, pontificating amusingly. After a meal, and with all attention riveted upon him, he related stories of his life.

The dear boy, dear Anthony, hasn't changed. He's not as tall as I expected, but it is evident that he was once a man of strength. Emphysema, through working in an asbestos factory in his youth, has robbed him of much of his physical power, but not his enthusiasm for life.

Anthony cried and laughed as he read this book. With a rage that seemed to enlarge his presence, he recalled incidents of ill-treatment at the Orphanage which were far more horrific than my own.

At the tender age of eight, for example, he was about to be beaten for the transgression of another, when he heard the laundry-cart horse stopping in the yard below the window. Fearing and remembering previous brutal lashes, he flung himself out of the first-floor window, with the intention of escaping by landing on the canvas hood of the cart. A moment's hesitation. The old horse moved off. Anthony plunged on to the cobbled ground and suffered a broken arm. However, he did escape the beating.

Soon after the arm had healed, a caterpillar was the cause of further strife. He had discovered it among his cabbage and refused to eat the greens. The cabbage, and nothing else, was placed in front of him for the best part of two days. To stop him fainting, he was given a bowl of porridge, then sent to the study of Dr Green for punishment.

Dr Green was leaving as Anthony arrived, and he told the boy to wait outside his room. It seemed an age passed, during which Anthony reflected with terror upon his fate. Would he get the dreaded birch or just the cane? A wild idea entered his head. Trembling he slipped inside the room and, in feverish haste, took up the poker from the side of the roaring fire, forced open the locked Welsh linen press in which were kept the instruments of torture, removed the various rods and threw them into the fire. That done, he turned to flee, and, before he could reach the door, was flung on to his back by a collision with the burly figure of the superintendent.

The impact made Dr Green furious. How dare Anthony enter his study without permission? Then his eyes lighted on the poker left on his desk. Anthony followed his gaze, to the fire, to the cupboard, and watched a state of apoplexy engulf the terrifying man. Dr Green approached him and spoke quietly. He was like a coiled cobra.

'What do you know of this?'

'I did it. I did it. I did it,' Anthony yelled.

'You admit it. By George, you admit it.'

Dr Green turned away and shuffled through the contents of the umbrella stand. He selected a stout walking stick. Grabbing hold of Anthony by the back of his neck and forcing him down upon the desk, the brute proceeded to thrash him until he became unconscious.

Anthony came round in the isolation ward of the infirmary,

lying face down on a cot, his hands tied to its sides so he could not turn over. His back was being painted yellow from his neck to the back of his knees.

Later he heard that there had been an annual inspection from the ladies and gentlemen of the school governors' committee. He was told that no one wanted to see him because he was such a bad boy, but he realised that he had been hidden in the isolation unit because explaining what had happened to him might have been a problem.

When he returned to the class, he was surprised to be called to the teacher's desk and given the pocket money he had missed through being bed-ridden. The boys got two farthings a week. Anthony is musical, like our father. He saved for a mouthorgan, and remembers the joy of handing over twenty-four hard-earned farthings for it.

The boys learned plumbing, carpentry and shoe-making in the Orphanage; they were also taught to make suet and bread puddings and to knit, darn and sew. It was clear that the Orphanage took in laundry from outside. Anthony grated up big bars of yellow soap, mixing them with soda and adding them to boiling water, and remembers washing fancy items, while I, in the sewing room, mended many a fine garment.

Boot-cleaning duty was a particularly nasty punishment, and was carried out in a tumble-down, draughty old shed. A great mound, higher than Anthony, of masters' and matrons' shoes and boys' boots, tied together with their laces, had to be cleaned and shone to perfection.

An enamel bowl filled with water, a big block of Day and Martin's boot-black, and an enormous brush were provided. The brush was dipped into the water, scraped across the block and rubbed into each boot, removing the scuff marks and producing a dull matte finish. One by one Anthony placed the boots on the other side. When the mound was totally transferred, he reversed the process. After drying the brush upon a sack, he polished the boots and shoes, with much effort, to a high shine and replenished the stack.

In the winter, the never-ending job was carried out by the light of two candles. As the night wore on, and his arms ached, he often saw the reflected eyes of the rats that scurried about. At this time he was learning about the Great Plague of London. He had awful visions of being bitten and dying at the tender age of nine, before anyone came for him.

Poor Anthony. When we had parted, all those years ago, running before the chase, he was caught and put in prison at Wormwood Scrubs. Lost, he was to spend many months awaiting trial. Finally he was sent to an approved school, escaped, and, after wandering the countryside, was apprehended and sent to a fine School of Forestry, which was disciplined but fair and where he got on well. Later he did national service in the Paratroopers. He did indeed eventually become an engineer. A fine fellow. He was widowed some eight years ago.

Our mother, it turned out, had been one of six children. They were all known by pet names: Boodles, Babs, Baby, Kitty, Sonney and Tiddles.

As a child I had no idea that the Hayes-Allen (Mother's maiden name) family was anything to do with us, but I do recall being given a letter and instructed to take it to an elegant house in Kensington. I was greeted by a maid who looked me up and down with some distaste, then banged the door in my face. I stood outside for some time, then wandered off and tore open the envelope.

The note read: *For the love of God, feed this child. Tiddles.*

I threw it away.

Mother had been born in Bangalore, India, pampered in early childhood, then banished to the harsh climate of an austere convent in England. An inordinately wilful child, she was beyond the understanding of those entrusted with her care. She did exceptionally well in her studies and later travelled extensively around Europe, furthering her education in Germany.

Her love of speed led her to a craze for motor cycles and fast cars, resulting in several severe accidents, which no doubt caused serious damage to her health. (Anthony recalls her driving him on a rare outing from the Orphanage in a red Morgan sports car with a long exposed engine.) She later joined a group of people who drifted around Europe seeking new ideas. The small allowance she received from her father came to an end and she supported herself by modelling. Her surprisingly small hands with their exquisitely manicured nails adorned advertisements for hand creams, mainly in Germany.

In England once again, she met James Hughes, who had a striking likeness to her beloved father. He was gentle and indulging; her sparkle enthralled him. They were married within a short time of their meeting. For a while happily if not competently ('I couldn't even boil an egg,' she said), she threw herself into motherhood.

Our father came from a mining family in Wales. His brothers worked hewing coal but he had won a scholarship to the Royal Academy of Music. Like many others, he had ended up playing with a small band instead of an orchestra. The precarious economic climate of 1931, and the advent of the radio, put many musicians in a desperate position. Finally, even the work at tawdry clubs ran out.

He was twenty years older than his wife, twenty years older than most other family men looking for work of any kind. He was a gentle, softly spoken Welshman who, from a boy, had been happy to escape the rigours of the mines, and had never been equipped to fight for a job.

Then he found himself with a young wife, four tiny children, and no money, no help, no food, no love left and no hope.

He committed suicide.

Indelible images remain with me of people who were kind to me. I thank you all, especially good Miss Cole and Miss Hamilton, the wise probation officer, both now gone, and the country policeman and his wife who, I am now convinced, saved my life on the road from Wales to London.

I think I know what I do. I can do a lot. Nobody told me I couldn't. An optimist and cheerful, I try not to pass judgement upon others. I endeavour to be fairly honest with those around me and more honest with myself, with whom I feel peaceful, loving and forgiving.

Then there is the future. I am content that my awareness has brought me bonuses, and I've been lucky enough to realise that life itself is magnificent, even with nothing beyond it.

I spend a few hours each day pondering over this and that while running the household, sometimes write a bit or make things. People tell me their troubles. I have moments of vulgarity, am a good cook and have green fingers. I am lucky, happy and I believe in the future of mankind, if not on this planet then out there somewhere among the stars, but not for me.

This book was born out of buried griefs and shames, now resolved.

It is dedicated to all those people, especially children, hurt and angry in circumstances beyond their control. Be patient, kind, forgiving, and be good, just for yourselves. I wish you understanding, happiness and peace, my friends, and some cake and jam.

Marian Hughes
London
January 1994